MODERN HUMANITIES RESEARCH ASSOCIATION

CRITICAL TEXTS

VOLUME 6

Editor
BRIAN RICHARDSON
(*Italian*)

DANTE ALIGHIERI
FOUR POLITICAL LETTERS

DANTE ALIGHIERI
FOUR POLITICAL LETTERS

Translated and with a commentary by

Claire E. Honess

MODERN HUMANITIES RESEARCH ASSOCIATION
2007

Published by

The Modern Humanities Research Association
1 Carlton House Terrace
London SW1Y 5DB

© The Modern Humanities Research Association, 2007

Claire E. Honess has asserted her right under the Copyright, Designs and Patents Act 1988 to be identified as the author of this work.

All rights reserved. No part of this publication may be reproduced, stored in a retrieval system, or transmitted, in any form or by any means, electronic, mechanical, photocopying, recording or otherwise, without the prior permission of the publishers.

First published 2007

ISBN 978-0-947623-70-8
ISSN 1746-1642

Copies may be ordered from www.criticaltexts.mhra.org.uk

Table of Contents

Preface 1

Acknowledgements ....…….................................. 3

Abbreviations 4

Introduction: 'Rome once had two suns' 5

The Letter to the Prince and Peoples of Italy (Letter V) 45

The Letter to the Florentines (Letter VI) 57

The Letter to the Emperor Henry VII (Letter VII) 69

The Letter to the Italian Cardinals (Letter XI) 83

Bibliography 99

Preface

This volume contains a translation of, and commentary on, four letters written by Dante Alighieri between 1310 and 1314 and having to do with key issues in contemporary politics. The letters are those conventionally numbered V, VI, VII, and XI in collections of Dante's letters, and focus on the Italian campaign of Henry VII (letters V, VI, and VII) and on the papal vacancy after the death of Pope Clement V (letter XI).

Letters V, VI, and VII are found (along with six more of the letters conventionally attributed to Dante) in a 1394 manuscript, Biblioteca Apostolica Vaticana, MS Palatino Latino 1729, produced for, and in part transcribed by, Francesco Piendibeni. The manuscript also contains Dante's *Monarchia* and Petrarch's *Bucolicum carmen*. Letters V and VII are also found in another manuscript from the second half of the fourteenth century (S. Pantaleo 8) in the Biblioteca Nazionale Centrale in Rome, and a further, late fifteenth-century, copy of letter VII is found in the Biblioteca Nazionale Marciana in Venice (MS Lat. XIV 115 (4710)). Letter XI exists in a single manuscript, held in the Biblioteca Medicea Laurenziana in Florence (Plut. XXIX 8). This manuscript, known as the 'Zibaldone Boccaccesco', was produced in around 1350 and contains copies of letters III, XI, and XII in Boccaccio's own hand.

The most recent English translation of all thirteen of the letters normally attributed to Dante was produced by Paget Toynbee in 1920: *Dantis Alagherii Epistolae: The Letters of Dante*, ed. by Paget Toynbee, 2nd edn (Oxford: Clarendon Press, 1966). Toynbee's edition is, first and foremost, however, a critical edition of the Latin text of the letters, and it is to the Latin text that all his footnotes refer. These notes focus above all on questions relating to the text of the letters and – particularly in the case of letter XI – on establishing the most plausible reading of problematic passages. Toynbee carefully identifies the biblical and classical sources referred to by Dante in his letters, but rarely offers further elucidation of the context and significance of these references. Moreover, the English of Toynbee's translation now feels seriously dated.

In 1954, a new translation (by Colin Hardie) of three of Dante's political letters (V, VI, and VII) appeared in the same volume as a translation of the *Monarchia*: Dante, *Monarchy and Three Political*

Letters, trans. by Donald Nicholl and Colin Hardie (London: Weidenfeld and Nicolson, 1954). This translation of the 'Henry VII' letters, which contains a bare minimum of notes, presents them more as an interesting appendix to the *Monarchia* than as works worthy of study in their own right, and the lack of notes means that their usefulness to readers of Dante's other works is very limited

This edition aims to provide a modern and accessible English translation of Dante's letters on political themes (and not only those relating to Henry VII), with an introduction and full explanatory commentary which shed light on the role of these letters not only as documents which emphasize and support the political views put forward most explicitly in the *Monarchia* and in book IV of the *Convivio*, but also as pieces of persuasive and impassioned writing which, on many different levels, reflect the concerns of the author's great poetic work, the *Commedia*.

The present translation is based on the Latin text of Dante's letters edited by Arsenio Frugoni: *Epistole*, ed. by Arsenio Frugoni and Giorgio Brugnoli, in Dante Alighieri, *Opere minori*, 2 vols (Milan and Naples: Ricciardi, 1979-88), II, 505-643. I have also made extensive use of Toynbee's edition, particularly in places where his reading of the text differs from that of Frugoni. Where my translation depends on Toynbee rather than Frugoni this is indicated in the notes.

Acknowledgements

Thanks are due to many people whose help and support have enabled me to complete this book. Zyg Barański, Richard Barraclough, Kate Ebisch-Burton, Danielle Hipkins, and Matthew Treherne have read all or parts of the text, which has benefited greatly from their wise and sensitive contributions. I am particularly grateful to Brian Richardson, Italian Editor of the Critical Texts series, for his invaluable advice. It goes without saying that responsibility for any remaining imperfections is wholly my own. I gratefully acknowledge receipt of a Faculty of Arts Study Leave Award from the University of Leeds, which enabled me to begin work on this project, and I am indebted to Mark Williams and Andrew Thompson for their institutional support, on behalf of the School of Modern Languages and Cultures and the Faculty of Arts, which has enabled me to complete it. I should also like to thank my colleagues, past and present, at the University of Leeds, whose enthusiasm and professionalism is an inspiration. Finally, a huge thank-you to Richard, Madeleine, and Ellen, who helped by just being themselves.

This book is dedicated to my parents, to whom I owe so much.

Abbreviations

The following abbreviations are used in the present volume (full references can be found in the Bibliography):

Conv.   Dante Alighieri, *Convivio*, ed. by Cesare Vasoli and Domenico De Robertis

DVE   Dante Alighieri, *De vulgari eloquentia*, ed. and trans. by Steven Botterill

Inf.   Dante Alighieri, *Inferno*, in *La Commedia secondo l'antica vulgata*, ed. by Giorgio Petrocchi

Mon.   Dante Alighieri, *Monarchia*, ed. and trans. by Prue Shaw

Par.   Dante Alighieri, *Paradiso*, in *La Commedia secondo l'antica vulgata*, ed. by Giorgio Petrocchi

Purg.   Dante Alighieri, *Purgatorio*, in *La Commedia secondo l'antica vulgata*, ed. by Giorgio Petrocchi

VN   Dante Alighieri, *Vita nuova*, ed. by Domenico De Robertis

Introduction: 'Rome once had two suns'

1. Dante's Letters

Thirteen Latin letters are traditionally attributed to Dante Alighieri,[1] although the authenticity of one of these, the famous letter to Cangrande della Scala, continues to be questioned by some commentators.[2] It appears likely, however, that Dante wrote more letters, which have not survived for posterity. This much is hinted at as early as the time of the *Vita nuova*, when Dante claims that he wrote a letter to the 'principi de la terra', describing the bereft state of Florence after the death of Beatrice (*VN*, XXX. 1). Boccaccio, in his *Trattatello in laude di Dante*, claims that Dante wrote 'molte Pìstole prosaiche in latino, delle quali ancora appariscono assai'.[3] Villani specifically mentions three letters by Dante:

> Quando fu in esilio [...] in tra·ll'altre fece tre nobili pistole; l'una mandò al reggimento di Firenze dogliendosi del suo esilio sanza colpa; l'altra mandò a lo 'mperadore Arrigo quand'era a l'assedio di Brescia,[4] riprendendolo della sua stanza, quasi profetezzando; la terza a' cardinali italiani, quand'era la vacazione dopo la morte di papa Chimento, accio chè s'accordassono a eleggere papa italiano; tutte in latino con alto dittato, e con eccellenti

---

[1] For a general introduction to Dante's letters, see Ahern, 'Epistles'; D'Entrèves, *Dante as a Political Thinker*, pp. 37-41 and 61-63; Mazzoni, 'Le epistole di Dante'; Morghen, 'Le lettere politiche di Dante' and 'La lettera di Dante ai Cardinali italiani'; Pastore Stocchi, 'Epistole'.

[2] It is not my intention in the present volume to discuss the letter to Cangrande (letter XIII in modern editions) in detail, nor to enter into the debate surrounding its genuineness. For a full discussion of the issue, see Barański, '*Comedìa*'; Barolini, 'For the Record'; Brugnoli, 'Introduzione'; Hall and Sowell, '*Cursus* in the Can Grande Epistle'; Hollander, *Dante's Epistle to Cangrande*; Kelly, *Tragedy and Comedy from Dante to Pseudo-Dante*; Pertile, '*Canto-cantica-Comedìa*'.

[3] Boccaccio, *Trattatello in laude di Dante*, p. 79.

[4] This is an inaccuracy. The letter to Henry VII is dated 17 April 1311, whereas the siege of Brescia did not begin until May that year.

sentenzie e autoritadi, le quali furono molto commendate da' savi intenditori.[5]

While the letters to the Emperor and to the Italian cardinals referred to by Villani can be identified with those conventionally numbered VII and XI in modern editions, the letter to the government of Florence regarding the poet's exile does not seem to have survived;[6] it may, however, be the same letter that is mentioned by Leonardo Bruni in his *Vita di Dante* of 1436:

> Cercando con buone opere e con buoni portamenti racquistar la grazia di poter tornare in Firenze per ispontanea revocazione di chi reggeva la terra [...] scrisse più volte non solamente a' particulari cittadini, ma ancora al popolo; ed intra l'altre un'epistola assai lunga, che incomincia, *Popule mi, quid feci tibi?*[7]

Bruni also mentions several other letters which have not survived, including one describing the battle of Campaldino, and two discussing Dante's role in Florentine politics before his exile (including his period as Prior), as well as referring to the letters to the wicked rulers of Florence (letter VI) and to Henry VII (letter VII). Indeed, in the fifteenth and sixteenth centuries various other letters were attributed to Dante, with greater or lesser degrees of plausibility, including letters to the King of Hungary, to Pope Boniface VIII, and to Guido da Polenta.[8]

Even restricting the focus, however, to those letters attributed with some degree of certainty to Dante and available in modern editions, it is clear that letter-writing represented an important mode of expression for the poet, and one in which he was able – at least in the most important of these texts – to adopt a striking and distinctive voice. The letters which have survived are extremely wide-ranging, in keeping with the breadth of the poet's interests

---

[5] Villani, *Nuova cronica*, X. 136.

[6] This letter cannot be identified with letter VI, which does indeed address the rulers of Florence, but in anger at their resistance to Henry VII rather than in sorrow at the author's exile.

[7] Bruni, *Le vite di Dante e del Petrarca*, p. 43.

[8] See Toynbee, *Epistolae*, pp. xxviii-xxxvi.

throughout his life and works. Both personal (expressing sorrow at his continued exile from Florence, for example) and formal (where the author speaks not in his own voice but as the spokesman for a group or for another individual),[9] they deal with the political and the poetic issues which were most important to Dante,[10] and offer a privileged insight into his views at key moments in his career. This is nowhere clearer than in the case of the four letters chosen for inclusion in this volume (V, VI, VII, and XI in modern editions). Clearly intended as 'open letters' – as 'political manifestoes',[11] far more than as pieces of personal correspondence –, these letters mark Dante's first attempt to engage with the most important large-scale political issues of his day in a practical way and, for the reader of Dante's better-known works, provide a deeper understanding of both the political theory of the *Monarchia* (and, to a lesser extent, the *Convivio*) and the political poetry of the *Commedia*.[12]

---

[9] More personal letters are the letters to Cino da Pistoia (III) and to an unnamed Florentine friend concerning a possible return from exile (XII). In contrast, letter I is addressed to Cardinal Niccolò da Prato on behalf of the exiled Florentine White Guelph faction, while letters VIII, IX, and X are addressed to Margaret of Brabant, the wife of Henry VII, on behalf of the wife of Count Guido di Battifolle, whose guest Dante appears to have been at the time of writing.

[10] The most famous letter dealing with poetic matters is, of course, that addressed to Cangrande della Scala (XIII), while letters III and IV – addressed to Cino da Pistoia and Moroello Malaspina respectively – both deal with questions related to love poetry and specifically with the question of whether one love can legitimately be replaced by another. The political letters will be dealt with in more detail below.

[11] Toynbee distinguishes between those of Dante's letters which were 'in the nature of political manifestoes' and those which were concerned, rather, with 'his own personal interests' (Toynbee, *Epistolae*, p. xiii). For Morghen, the letters contained in this volume belong less to the genre of 'epistolografia' than to that of 'pubblicistica politica' ('La lettera di Dante ai Cardinali italiani', p. 112), while Ferrante describes them as 'undisguised political propaganda' (*Political Vision*, p. 108).

[12] For an argument that the *Commedia* needs to be seen as a 'political' text in a very broad sense, which stretches far beyond the limited number of passages traditionally identified as dealing with matters of politics, see my *From Florence to the Heavenly City*.

2. Dante and Politics

The poet had, of course, engaged in practical political activity in the years preceding his exile from Florence. From the time of the relaxing of the Ordinances of Justice in 1295,[13] Dante played an active part in the government of his city. He sat on various Florentine councils, he acted as the city's envoy to neighbouring San Gimignano, and between June and August 1300 he served a period as Prior. Dante's Priorate fell at a particularly turbulent time in Florence's history, and indeed, if the letter on the subject quoted by Bruni is genuine, it would seem that the poet identified this period as lying at the root of all his later political troubles: 'Tutti li mali, e [tutti] l'inconvenienti miei dalli infausti comizi del mio priorato ebbono cagione e principio'.[14] It seems likely that the decisions which Dante took at this time, along with his outspoken resistance, a year later, to the city's plans to supply horsemen to serve the Pope, would have sealed his fate in the eyes of his political opponents and rendered inevitable his banishment from the city.[15] This involvement in the day-to-day running of Florentine affairs was, however, primarily local in outlook, and was abruptly curtailed by the sentence of exile passed on the poet in 1301 and confirmed in 1302.

---

[13] The Ordinances of Justice (*Ordinamenti di giustizia*) barred 'magnates' (Florentines from noble families) from holding office in the city, and consolidated power primarily in the hands of the guilds. In 1295, the conditions of the Ordinances of Justice were made slightly less stringent, enabling members of the minor nobility (like Dante himself) to participate in government, provided that they became a member of a guild. Dante enrolled, at this time, in the guild of Physicians and Apothecaries, an action which seems to mark the beginning of his active involvement in politics. On the politics of this period in Florence, see Larner, *Italy in the Age of Dante and Petrarch*, pp. 106-25; Martines, 'Political Violence in the Thirteenth Century'; Salvemini, *Magnati e popolani*; Waley, *The Italian City Republics*, pp. 117-56.

[14] Bruni, *Le vite di Dante e del Petrarca*, p. 36. Although it seems likely that the original letter would have been written, like all Dante's surviving letters, in Latin, Bruni apparently quotes from it (emphasizing the veracity of his quotation by adding 'queste sono le parole sue') in Italian, the language in which his *Vita* is written.

[15] On the life of Dante, see: Bemrose, *A New Life of Dante*; Cosmo, *Vita di Dante*; Mazzotta, 'Life of Dante'; Petrocchi, *Vita di Dante*; Scott, *Understanding Dante*, pp. 316-20.

INTRODUCTION

Evidence of a more narrowly 'municipal' political perspective can also be found in the earliest of the extant letters attributed to Dante. This letter is addressed to Cardinal Niccolò da Prato, who had been appointed 'peace-maker' in Tuscany by Pope Benedict XI and who had entered Florence on 10 March 1304. It is written on behalf of the whole exiled Florentine White Guelph faction and its author is never explicitly named, although its traditional attribution to Dante has not been challenged.[16] In this letter, the political aims of Dante, and of his fellow-exiles, extend no further than a return to Florence. The Whites' sole desire, in their exile, is that healing ('patrie sanitatem') be brought to their city, and the letter's principal recurring theme is that of the desire for peace: a peace which will allow the exiles to return and civil rights to be restored.[17] Political events beyond those directly affecting the vicissitudes of Florence and its citizens (whether within the city or excluded from it) are absent from Dante's sphere of interest here.

If, in 1304, Dante's political universe was still predominantly Florentine, this was soon to change, however, with his breaking away from the 'compagnia malvagia e scempia' (*Par.*, XVII. 62) of his fellow-exiles. The fourth book of the *Convivio*, written around 1306, already reflects the strongly pro-imperial point of view which will be put forward in the later political letters. The poet's commentary on his *canzone* 'Le dolci rime d'amor', with its theme of 'true nobility', serves as the pretext for a discussion of the perfect form of human society. Drawing on the political ideas of both Aristotle and St Augustine, Dante asserts that 'l'uomo naturalmente è compagnevole animale',[18] but that since 'l'animo umano in terminata possessione di terra non si queti, ma sempre

---

[16] On the attribution of this letter to Dante, see Toynbee, *Epistolae*, pp. 2-3.

[17] 'For the healing of our city, which we have longed for as if dreaming in our desire for it, is promised to us more than once in your letter, beneath the fatherly admonitions. Why else did we rush into a civil war? What else did our white standards seek? And why else did our swords and spears turn red, except to ensure that those whose rash desires have destroyed civil rights submit their necks to the yoke of the holy laws and work together for the peace of the city. Indeed, the legitimate arrow of our intentions, springing from the bow which we held, sought only the peace and freedom of the Florentine people; we seek this, and will always do so. [...] Therefore we beg your most merciful holiness with filial voices and with great affection to nourish with the calm of tranquillity and peace this Florence which has been tormented for so long' (letter I. 2-4; my translation).

[18] Compare Aristotle, *Politics*, I. 2: 'man is by nature a political animal'.

desideri gloria d'acquistare', peace in human relations can never be achieved, unless there be a 'Monarchia'; that is, 'uno principato, e uno prencipe [...] lo quale, tutto possedendo e più desiderare non possendo, li regi tegna contenti ne li termini de li regni, sì che pace intra loro sia, ne la quale si posino le cittadi, e in questa posa le vicinanze s'amino, in questo amore le case prendano ogni loro bisogno, lo qual preso, l'uomo viva felicemente' and the fundamental human political inclination is satisfied (*Conv.*, IV. iv. 2-4). This argument is the same one that will be put forward later in the *Monarchia*,[19] and expressed poetically in the *Commedia*, and it provides the theoretical basis for many of the views which Dante expresses in the letters collected in this volume. A universal monarchy is necessary, Dante argues, in order to guarantee the peaceful co-existence of human beings on earth as 'political animals'; and that universal monarchy – he goes on – must necessarily take the form of a specifically Roman empire, since the entire history of Rome proves that the city has been divinely predestined for this role.[20] Moreover, this imperial ideal is a wholly secular one, quite separate from the spiritual role of the Church in saving souls. Neither the *Convivio* nor the *Monarchia*, however, is a work of practical politics. In these texts Dante speaks in purely theoretical terms; he is concerned to identify *the best* form of human society, rather than to respond to a real political situation, and the personal dimension which comes to the fore in the political letters is here almost totally absent.[21]

In these letters, therefore, we witness the coming-together for the first time of Dante the political *theorist* and Dante the political *activist*. His point of view here is no longer restricted to political affairs within the city-walls of Florence; yet it is, equally, not purely theoretical, in so far as he is addressing a very specific set of political circumstances affecting both Church and State, and not

---

[19] The dating of the *Monarchia* has been much discussed. Most commentators now take at face value the reference to *Paradiso* V in book I, chapter 12, and therefore agree that the work must have been written after 1314.

[20] See *Convivio*, IV. v and *Monarchia*, II.

[21] Anthony Cassell comments on the apparent 'aloofness' of the *Monarchia*, noting Dante's 'tactic of shrouding any reference to immediate contemporary affairs' and his attempt 'to create the impression of a message beyond time, derived from man's divine reason and inspired by God's revelation' (Cassell, 'Monarchia', pp. 616-17).

merely an imagined ideal. It is my aim in this introduction to show how these letters relate both to the precise historical situation in which they were written and to Dante's *œuvre* as a whole. In particular, I shall explore the connections which can be identified between these letters (written in prose and in Latin) and the vernacular political poetry of the *Commedia*, in particular, on the level of their deeply religious and prophetic inspiration.

3. The Political Letters

Letters V, VI, and VII are closely linked and, in fact, are often considered as a group (sometimes labelled simply 'Dante's political letters').[22] They all relate directly to the Italian campaign of the Emperor Henry VII, and express Dante's intense hopes for a restoration of the great Roman Empire of the past in the figure of Henry, who is portrayed consistently as Italy's saviour, a new Messiah, who will resolve all the political difficulties caused by the wars and factionalism which plague the peninsula, and particularly the city-states of Northern and Central Italy. Henry, Duke of Luxembourg, had been chosen as King of the Romans and Emperor-elect on 27 November 1308, and crowned by the Archbishop of Cologne on 6 January 1309.[23] Only a coronation in Rome, however, could confirm Henry's imperial authority, and in autumn 1310 he set out for Italy, crossing the Alps on 23 October. Dante's letter to the 'Princes and Peoples of Italy' (V) dates from this period, and announces Henry's arrival in Italy with undisguised joy and hope for the future: 'Now is the time for you to rejoice, Italy [...], because your bridegroom, the world's

---

[22] See, for example, the Nicholl and Hardie translation, which is entitled *Monarchy and Three Political Letters*. My inclusion of the letter to the Italian Cardinals in the present volume represents an attempt to broaden the focus of our understanding of Dante's political thought to include the Church as well as the Empire. Other letters by Dante could equally well be termed political; the letter to Niccolò da Prato (letter I) has already been mentioned, but is not included in this volume because it is in the nature of a 'party statement', rather than expressing Dante's personal views in his own authentic 'voice'. Catherine Keen has also argued convincingly for a political reading of letter IV (and of the poem which it accompanies and discusses, 'Amor da che convien pur ch'io mi doglia') (Keen, 'Addressing the City').

[23] See Bowsky, *Henry VII in Italy*, p. 19. Henry's 'German' coronation of 1309 would be confirmed by his 'Lombard' coronation in Milan in 1311, and finally by his 'imperial' coronation in Rome on 29 June 1312.

comforter and glory of your people, that most merciful Henry, holy Augustus and Caesar, is hurrying to his wedding' (V. 2). This hope was to be short-lived, however. After an enthusiastic reception in northern Italy and a coronation ceremony in Milan which served to increase Henry's credibility with many Italians,[24] Henry failed to proceed swiftly south down the peninsula and to ensure a timely coronation in Rome. By spring 1311, when Dante wrote letters VI and VII,[25] Henry's journey to Rome had apparently stalled in the face of strong opposition from Florence and her allies, combined with a series of delaying tactics on the part of Pope Clement V. In letter VI, therefore, Dante vehemently attacks the rulers of Florence (the 'most wicked Florentines within the city'), upbraiding them for their continued resistance to Henry and warning them of the dire consequences which (he imagines) will result from their attempts to prevent Henry from taking on his divinely willed role. And in letter VII, in his frustration that the momentum of the autumn and winter seems to have been lost, Dante turns to Henry himself in a letter which mixes acclamation and disappointment, criticizing his apparent inactivity while reasserting his faith in Henry's quasi-messianic imperial mission.

Letter XI, written in 1314 after the death of Pope Clement V, deals not with the Empire, but with that other great medieval political (as well as spiritual) authority, the Church. Critics have not, hitherto, emphasized the thematic and stylistic links between this letter and the three letters relating to Henry VII's Italian campaign. The letters are connected, however, by a preoccupation with the specifically Roman heritage and destiny of the institution in question. Just as Dante had urged Henry (the man chosen by God to take on the role of the universal sovereign) to proceed with all possible haste to Rome (the place chosen by God as the seat of such a universal monarchy), so too does Dante, in this letter, urge the Italian cardinals, meeting in the conclave at Carpentras to elect Clement's successor, to choose a Pope who will return the Papacy

---

[24] The coronation in Milan took place on 6 January 1311, exactly two years after Henry's original coronation in Aachen cathedral. Regarding the significance of the Milan coronation, Bowsky comments that '[d]espite the vagueness of the Italian coronation tradition, the rites in Milan helped make this French-speaking ruler from north of the Alps more acceptable to certain Italians' (*Henry VII in Italy*, p. 82).

[25] Letter VI is dated 31 March 1311; letter VII is dated 17 April of the same year.

to its rightful place in Rome. The Pope, just as much as the Emperor, derives legitimacy, in Dante's eyes, from the place in which his authority resides, the place 'which was consecrated as the Apostolic See by Peter himself and by Paul, the Apostle to the Gentiles, through the shedding of their own blood' (XI. 2).

The Papacy's removal by Clement V to Avignon – where it looked likely to stay unless decisive action were taken at Carpentras – along with the vacancy of the Empire after the death of Henry VII left Rome 'deprived of both her lights' (XI. 10), in a phrase which is strikingly reminiscent of Marco Lombardo's description of Rome in *Purgatorio* XVI:

> 'Soleva Roma, che 'l buon mondo feo,
> due soli aver, che l'una e l'altra strada
> facean vedere, e del mondo e di Deo.'
> (*Purg.*, XVI. 106-08)

Dante's point, in the *Purgatorio*, is that Church and Empire should be constituted as equal but separate authorities, the one lighting the spiritual path, the other the secular, in direct refutation of Boniface VIII's famous Bull, *Unam sanctam*, which had argued that secular authority must always and necessarily be subject to spiritual authority.[26] In the letter, Dante does not explicitly compare the roles of Empire and Papacy, as he does in the *Commedia*. Yet it is clear that here too he is concerned to show the negative consequences of one light having extinguished the other ('L'un l'altro ha spento'; *Purg.*, XVI. 109), leaving Christians on earth without the guidance which they need in order to keep to the 'diritta via' of a properly ordered life on earth: 'You, whose duty it was to light the way of your faithful flock through the wood of this earthly pilgrimage, have led your followers and yourselves to the very edge of the precipice' (XI. 4).[27] Moreover, in the image of

---

[26] As Joan Ferrante explains, *Unam Sanctam* claims 'a divine hierarchy in which spiritual power excels any earthly power in dignity and nobility [...]; the spiritual power can judge the earthly, whereas only God can judge the spiritual' (*Political Vision*, pp. 79-80).

[27] This passage clearly recalls *Inferno* I as well as *Purgatorio* XVI; the consequence of a lack of guidance in the political and religious spheres can only be, as Marco Lombardo makes abundantly clear, the sin symbolized by the Dark Wood into which Dante's pilgrim has wandered at the beginning of the

Rome's two 'lights', Dante hints that his view of the relationship between the Papacy and the Empire has developed in the three years since he wrote letter VI, in which he sarcastically asks the Florentines who oppose the emperor and claim the right to self-government, 'If you would like to see two moons in the sky, why not also two suns?' (VI. 2). In the earlier letter Dante seems to accept the traditional identification of the Empire with the moon and the Papacy with the sun,[28] and, to assert the impossibility – the absurdity, even – of any alternative astronomical comparison. John Scott argues that it may have been precisely the events of 1312 and 1313, and specifically the betrayal of Henry VII by Clement V,[29] which changed Dante's views on this, and let him to formulate the striking and memorable image used in *Purgatorio* XVI, which he suggests may have been written at around the same time as book III of the *Monarchia* and letter XI.[30] This probable dating, along with the importance – in the context of Dante's *œuvre* as a whole – of viewing the Church and the Empire (whether construed as sun and moon or as two 'equal' suns) together as a key nexus within the poet's political thought, justifies the inclusion of letter XI in the present volume.

Commedia: 'la mala condotta | è la cagion che il mondo ha fatto reo, | e non natura che in voi sia corrotta' (*Purg.*, XVI. 103-05).

[28] See also letter V. 10 (and note 47 to letter V in this edition), where again Dante seems not to question the traditional view.

[29] In the period preceding Henry's coronation in Rome (29 June 1312), Clement had increasingly distanced himself from the Emperor-elect, linking himself more and more closely with Henry's opponent Robert of Anjou, King of Naples.

[30] See Scott, *Dante's Political Purgatory*, pp. 154-55. Nicolò Mineo suggests, in relation to the dating of the notion of the 'two suns' that 'qualcosa sembra esser cambiato nel breve intervallo tra la sesta e la settima lettera [...]. In questa infatti Enrico è chiamato decisamente "sol" e non ci sono riferimenti al rapporto sole-luna' (Mineo, 'Mondo classico e città terrena in Dante', p. 69). Mineo does not, however, mention the use of the image of Rome's two 'lights' in letter XI. Hollander, however, assumes that Dante has already formulated the notion of the Empire and Papacy as equal and separate 'lights' by the time of writing letter V, and that his apparently 'conventional' reference to the sun and moon here is no more than a sop to Clement V in the hope of sustaining his support for the Emperor: 'Dante even allows Clement's formulation of the two *luminaria* [...] to stand unchallenged [...]. But as the concluding words of the epistle make clear, Dante is concerned with the limitations that the forces of the "greater light" might place upon those of the lesser' (*Dante*, p. 134).

INTRODUCTION

The four letters translated here do not only share thematic concerns, however. They are also linked stylistically, and in particular through their heavy reliance on Biblical quotation and allusion.[31] As various commentators have emphasized, it is important that the rhetorical impact of these letters should not be underestimated.[32] Written in a style which conforms to the rules of the *ars dictaminis*, the medieval art of letter-writing, their 'literary' status has sometimes been questioned;[33] yet they seem to be more than just formulaic re-workings of a series of rhetorical conventions. And this is important, for, as Lino Pertile pointedly asks, conveniently problematizing this issue: if the letters can be dismissed as no more than examples of 'a special genre developed by lawyers in the service of popes, kings and emperors', 'does this mean that we cannot and must not take them seriously except as literary exercises in the marginal tradition of medieval letter-writing? That Dante in other words did not mean what he wrote?' (Pertile, 'Dante Looks Forward and Back, p. 1). The content of the letters clearly belies this latter suggestion. The letters are obviously heartfelt – they could hardly be more so – and their rhetoric, as Pertile concludes, 'is not employed by Dante to show what a consummate writer he is, but to persuade his readers of his arguments' (Pertile, 'Dante Looks Forward and Back', p. 5). Likewise, Raffaello Morghen asserts that 'non bisogna attribuire al carattere formale di queste composizioni tale rilievo da considerarle quasi mere esercitazioni retoriche'.[34]

---

[31] Mineo comments that 'le quattro lettere [...] presentano analogie, nel modo di strutturare la loro tematica, con brani messianici, comminatorii, ammonitorii degli scritti profetici' (Mineo, *Profetismo e apocalittica*, pp. 144-45).

[32] Writing of letter V, Hollander describes it as 'written at a rhetorical pitch that takes one's breath away' (*Dante*, p. 133), while Pertile talks of the 'inaudita violenza oratoria' of the letters relating to Henry VII (Pertile, *La puttana e il gigante*, p. 14).

[33] Ahern, for example, suggests that 'Dante's epistles were never intended to be read together (or separately) as literary texts' ('Epistles', p. 353). While it is certainly true that the letters do not form a coherent 'whole' as a literary work (and were never intended to do so by their author), this introduction will endeavour to show that there *is* a coherence that binds at least some of the letters, and that they certainly do have literary interest in their own right.

[34] Morghen, 'La lettera di Dante ai Cardinali italiani', p. 112. It is, rather, according to Morghen, the fact that these letters were copied into formularies and held up as examples of the 'bello stile cancelleresco' to be imitated by *later*

4. The 'Favourable Time' and the Messianic Emperor

While it may be true, therefore, that the letters' 'obsessive recourse to biblical citations and allusions is [...] the norm in imperial and ecclesiastical writings' (Pertile, 'Dante Looks Forward and Back', p. 1), the use of biblical language is here anything but casual. This much is clear from the opening words of the first of the letters under consideration, which proclaim, in a quotation from St Paul's second letter to the Corinthians that 'now is the favourable time' (V. 1). But, as is so often the case in Dante, the reader is not expected merely to take these words at face value; the notion of the 'favourable time' is not merely a rhetorical 'flourish', meant simply to suggest that the political problems of Italy will be resolved by the arrival of Henry VII.[35] Rather, an examination of the context of Dante's quotation of Paul suggests a more specific interpretation. In Paul's letter, this 'favourable time' is linked precisely with the mission of Christ and his first followers. Exhorting the members of the Church in Corinth not to neglect the grace which God has shown them and to continue to work tirelessly towards the goals of righteousness, St Paul reassures them that, if it is written that *'at the favourable time, I have listened to you; on the day of salvation I came to your help'*, then they can take comfort in the fact that 'now is the favourable time; this is the day of salvation' (II Corinthians 6. 2). This reassurance is, in turn, a reference to a prophecy found in the book of Isaiah, which foretells a coming time of peace, a time when freedom will be restored to the world: 'At the favourable time I will answer you, on the day of salvation I will help you. [...] I will restore the land and assign you the estates that lie waste. I will say to the prisoners, "Come out", to those who are in darkness, "Show yourselves"' (Isaiah 49. 8-9). This movement from darkness to light and from captivity to freedom, present in the passage from Isaiah which lies behind Dante's opening quotation, then provides the unifying thread which runs throughout the first paragraph of this letter. With the arrival of Henry VII, 'a new day is breaking

---

writers, that makes them seem so typical and, to some extent, disguises their originality and novelty.

[35] 'L'attacco dantesco, "Ecce nunc tempus acceptabile", non si può ridurre all'*ars* di una suggestiva formula retorica' (Rigo, *Memoria classica e memoria biblica*, p. 40).

and the light of that dawn is now allaying the shadows of our long period of adversity [...] The sky is glowing red to its farthest reaches and its gentle calm is inspiring hope in all people' (V. 1). Henry himself is described as Titan – the sun – whose dawning will restore justice to the world, who will take pity on 'the lamentations of [Italy's] universal captivity' and who, like another Moses, 'will deliver his people from their Egyptian oppression and lead them to a land flowing with milk and honey' (V. 1). The 'hidden' reference to Isaiah, which lies behind the overt quotation from Paul, thus enables Dante to draw a comparison between Italy and Israel, which will recur throughout the letter.[36]

Henry is not only, however, a 'new Moses' – able to transform the wilderness of contemporary Italy into a Promised Land –, he is also described in overtly messianic terms as 'the great Lion of the tribe of Judah',[37] and this identification is confirmed by the echo at the beginning of paragraph 2 of the letter of the *Nunc dimittis*. Just as Simeon identifies the baby Jesus as 'a light to enlighten the pagans and the glory of your people Israel' (Luke 2. 31-32), Henry – already portrayed, as has been seen, as a bringer of light – is 'the glory of [Italy's] people' (V. 2).[38] Moreover, in an image which explicitly recalls the Song of Songs and which again has strongly Christological implications, Henry is also compared to a bridegroom, hastening to be joined with his beloved.[39] As is well-known, one of the standard exegetical interpretations of the erotic love of the Bridegroom of the Song of Songs for his Bride was as

---

[36] See Di Scipio, *Pauline Thought*, p. 146; Pertile, 'Dante Looks Forward and Back', p. 8.

[37] This denomination too spans Old and New Testaments. In the Old Testament the 'Lion of the tribe of Judah' is consistently used to designate the hoped-for Messiah, and this is made explicit in Revelation 5, where 'the Lion of the tribe of Judah, the Root of David' is identified with the Lamb who is 'worthy to take the scroll and break the seals of it' because it was 'sacrificed, and with [its] blood [...] bought men for God of every race, language, people and nation' (Revelation 5. 5-9).

[38] See also Ferrante, *Political Vision*, p. 102.

[39] The relevance of this comparison is confirmed by the use of the Latin 'pulcerrima' ('most beautiful one') for Italy in the next sentence of Dante's letter. In the Song of Songs, the Bride is described as 'pulchra inter mulieres' or 'loveliest of women' (Song of Songs 1. 7 [1. 8 in modern editions]).

the love of Christ for his Church;[40] yet another analogy is therefore drawn between Henry and Christ, and 'the wedding between Henry and Italy is meant to re-enact the mystical union of Christ and the Church'.[41]

Indeed, the significance of the Song of Songs in Dante's letters may go much further than this. Both Nasti and Pertile have argued that the Titan image of paragraph 1 of this letter may be more than just another reference to Henry as the sun. Rather, they suggest that this image links Henry with another biblical passages which has strong connections with the Song of Songs and which was also interpreted in a messianic vein. Psalm 18 describes the sun as a bridegroom who comes out of his pavilion, exulting like a giant.[42] The reference to the bridegroom means that this passage was inevitably linked by exegetes to the Song of Songs, and the giant was seen as a figure of Christ, like the Bridegroom of the Song, and like Dante's Titan-Henry.[43] And, as Nasti goes on to argue, this identification seems to be confirmed in letter VII, when Henry is once again referred to as a Titan: 'when you, the successor of Caesar and of Augustus, bounded over the Apennines to return the revered Roman standards, immediately our deep sighs stopped and our flood of tears dried up; and, like the rising of a much-desired sun [literally, Titan] new hope for a better age for Italy shone out' (VII. 1). Here the image of the Emperor 'bounding' across the Apennines clearly recalls the Bride's description of her Bridegroom in the Song of Songs: 'I hear my Beloved. See how he comes leaping on the mountains, bounding over the hills' (Song of Songs 2. 8). Thus, 'anche Enrico, come lo sposo-Cristo, conquista

---

[40] On the Song of Songs in the Middle Ages, see Matter, *'The Voice of My Beloved'*; Nasti, *Favole d'amore*, pp. 15-41; Pertile, *La puttana e il gigante*, pp. 26-42.

[41] Pertile, 'Dante Looks Forward and Back', p. 8. See also Mazzotta, *Dante, Poet of the Desert*, p. 133, n. 41.

[42] Psalm 18 in the Vulgate corresponds to that numbered 19 in modern editions of the Psalms. The Latin *gigas* is sometimes translated as 'strong man' or 'hero' in English translations of this psalm.

[43] 'Titan [...] is not only the sun, but also the Giant of Psalm 18 [...]. Here [...] he is the a figure of the new messiah, who is about to arrive on the stage of the world, the bringer of peace and restorer of justice' (Pertile, 'Dante Looks Forward and Back', p. 7). See also, Nasti, *Favole d'amore*, pp. 143-45; Pertile, *La puttana e il gigante*, pp. 205-25.

e salta le vette per portare speranza e pace, anche lui è *salus* e redenzione dell'umanità derelitta' (Nasti, *Favole d'amore*, p. 145).

5. The City of God and the City of Man

These references combine in a striking accumulation of biblical, and specifically messianic, images in the opening paragraphs of letter V, which suggests that, when Dante announces the new time of 'peace and solace' that will be ushered in by Henry's arrival in Italy, he is thinking of something more substantial and more significant than merely the imposition of some sort of truce on Italy's warring factions by a stronger power. As we have seen, Dante believes that peace in the political sphere is rendered impossible, in the absence of a universal Monarch, by the 'gloria d'acquistare' (*Conv.*, IV. iv. 3) which inevitably taints all human relations. This political pessimism seems to be derived from the views of St Augustine, for whom post-lapsarian humanity is inevitably characterized by *cupiditas* (not just greed for possessions, but any kind of immoderate desire or ambition) and by the *libido dominandi* (or lust for power and desire for domination over others). For Augustine the *libido dominandi* has its roots in the sin of pride, which lies at the basis of the sin of Lucifer and that of Adam and Eve. Sinful human beings are seen as wanting to elevate themselves to the status of gods by lording it over their fellows, the people who should be their equals,[44] and this leads to a situation in the world where political authority has to be constituted to maintain a semblance of peace and order, using coercive force (whether overt or otherwise) to clamp down on the coercive force which citizens would otherwise use against one another.[45] This leads to Augustine's famous remark that earthly kingdoms are not so very different from bands of robbers,[46] and to his assertion that the only purpose of the secular state is that, under its control, 'unprincipled men are deprived of the freedom to do wrong with impunity' (*City of God*, XIX. 21). For Dante, however, the

---

[44] See Deane, *The Political Ideas of St Augustine*, p. 49.

[45] See Paolucci, *The Political Writings of St Augustine*, p. xvi.

[46] 'Remove justice, and what are kingdoms but gangs of criminals on a large scale? What are criminal gangs but petty kingdoms?' (*City of God*, IV. 4).

Emperor's role seems to be a much more significant one than simply that of controlling potential evil-doers – of being the world's policeman – and the peace which he believes can be achieved under a universal Emperor is more than just the absence of the war and discord which would otherwise be rife in human society. Rather, Dante implies that Henry's putative empire will bring together elements of Augustine's 'City of God' (the ideal community of the blessed in Heaven) within the City of Man (the temporal community of human beings on earth), bringing with it a peace which is not the fragile peace which can be engineered by human beings, but the true and lasting peace that comes directly from God.

In support of this view, Dante claims, in the letter to the Princes and Peoples of Italy, that Henry's authority comes not from his human electors but from God, once again bolstering his arguments with a series of biblical quotations. Thus, in the letter's fourth paragraph he addresses the Lombards, imploring them to accept Henry as their legitimate ruler. He urges them not to allow themselves to be seduced by the ploys of that cupidity ('cupiditas', 'gloria d'acquistare') which, as he had already claimed in the *Convivio*, lies at the root of all political discord, but to declare their obedience to Henry immediately, bearing in mind that 'anyone who resists authority is rebelling against God's decision' (V. 4). This injunction is a direct quotation from St Paul's letter to the Romans, and is taken from a passage which is wholly devoted to the relationship between secular and religious authorities:

> You must all obey the governing authorities. Since all government comes from God, the civil authorities were appointed by God, and so anyone who resists authority is rebelling against God's decision, and such an act is bound to be punished. Good behaviour is not afraid of magistrates; only criminals have anything to fear. If you want to live without being afraid of authority, you must live honestly and authority may even honour you. The state is there to serve God for your benefit. If you break the law, however, you may well have fear: the bearing of the sword has its significance. The authorities are there to serve God: they carry out God's revenge by punishing wrongdoers. You must obey, therefore, not only because

you are afraid of being punished, but also for conscience' sake. (Romans 13. 1-5)

Augustine's view that the purpose of the state is to punish wrongdoers only partially reflects Paul's argument here. The state, for Paul, does have a coercive function; but it also derives its authority from God, and as such is owed the respect and obedience of its Christian citizens.[47] In his letter to the Romans, St Paul – as Giuseppe Di Scipio points out – is claiming 'a universal role for Christianity, which could only be obtained through the evangelization of the Roman Empire, away from the provincialism of Palestine' (*Pauline Thought*, p. 149). Dante turns this around, in his letter, to claim a universal role for the Empire, which could only be obtained by the acceptance of imperial authority over the whole of Christendom, away from the provincialism of the Italian city-states. Through his quotation of Paul, Dante shows that there is good scriptural authority for believing that the state can (even if it does not always) act as an intermediary between the citizen and God.

The seriousness with which Dante takes this, is underlined by his immediate recourse to another biblical quotation, this time from the Acts of the Apostles. Asserting the futility of any resistance to Henry, Dante tells his readers that 'anyone who rebels against God's decisions is kicking out against an omnipotent will, and "it is hard to kick against the goad" ' (V. 4). The reference in this case is to the conversion of St Paul on the road to Damascus:

> I was going to Damascus [...] and at midday as I was on my way [...] I saw a light brighter than the sun come down from heaven. It shone brilliantly round me and my fellow travellers. We all fell to the ground, and I heard a voice saying to me in Hebrew, 'Saul, Saul, why are you persecuting me? It is hard to kick against the goad'. Then I said: Who are you, Lord? And the Lord answered, 'I am Jesus, and you are persecuting me. But get up and stand on your feet, for I have appeared to you for this reason: to appoint you as my servant and as witness of this vision in which you have seen me, and of others in which I shall

---

[47] On Paul and Augustine in this letter, see also Di Scipio, *Pauline Thought*, pp. 148-49.

appear to you. I shall deliver you from the people and
from the pagans, to whom I am sending you to open their
eyes, so that they may turn from darkness to light'. (Acts
26. 12-18)

The parallels here are clear. Those who resist the Emperor-elect are like Saul, who persecutes not only the early Christians, but also, by extension, Christ himself ('I am Jesus, and you are persecuting me'), while Henry is yet again with Christ and with the bringing of light to those living in darkness.

Later in the letter too, Dante adduces further biblical sources to emphasize the divinely willed nature of Henry's authority. In paragraph 7, he quotes Psalm 94 – 'the sea belongs to God and he made it, so does the land, he shaped this too' (Psalm 94. 5 [95. 5]) – in order to draw attention to the universality of Henry's dominion. This same passage is also used by Dante, and to very similar effect, in book III of the *Monarchia*:

> But Christ renounced this [earthly] kind of kingdom in the presence of Pilate, saying: 'My kingdom is not of this world; if my kingdom were of this world, then would my servants fight, that I should not be delivered to the Jews; but now is my kingdom not from hence'.[48] Which is not to be understood to mean that Christ, who is God, is not Lord of this kingdom, for the Psalmist says 'The sea is his, and he made it: and his hands formed the dry land'; but that, as the model for the church, he had no concern for this kingdom. (*Mon.*, III. xv. 5-6)

The conventional explanation of Christ's statement to Pilate to the effect that his kingdom is not of this world, is here countered by Dante's explanation that, far from meaning that Christ himself is not concerned with the political and social well-being of Christians on earth, his response to Pilate means only that the Church should not concern itself with political matters.

As we have seen, at the time of writing letter V Dante's views on the separation of the respective authorities of Church and State had not developed to the point that they later would in the

---

[48] See John 18. 36.

Monarchia (and in letter XI and *Purgatorio* XVI). In 1310, Roman authority – spiritual and secular – could still be represented for Dante by a sun and a moon, rather than by the striking image of 'Rome's two suns'. Nonetheless, Dante's view that loyalty to a spiritual authority (the Church) was not mutually exclusive with loyalty to the secular authority of the Empire was already clear, and is clearly expressed in paragraphs 9 and 10 of letter V. Dante first alludes to Christ's famous reply to the Pharisees, who had asked him whether it was permissible to pay taxes to Rome – 'Give back to Caesar what belongs to Caesar – and to God what belongs to God' (Matthew 22. 21) – and he then goes onto reiterate that the authority of the state comes from God, through a reference to the same conversation with Pilate that Dante would later cite in *Monarchia*, III. xv. When Jesus tells Pilate: 'You would have no power over me [...] if it had not been given you from above' (John 19. 11), he is asserting, not that imperial power is dependent on the spiritual authority of God's representatives on earth (the Church), but that imperial power is derived directly from the divine omnipotence of God; and this is illustrated strikingly in the letter's final biblical allusion. St Peter himself, the first Pope, is the authority here, making it difficult not to see, in his endorsement of Empire, an acceptance of what Dante would later present as the distinct and clearly defined orbits of the two institutions:

> For the sake of the Lord, accept the authority of every social institution: the emperor, as the supreme authority, and the governors as commissioned by him to punish criminals and praise good citizenship. God wants you to be good citizens, so as to silence what fools are saying in their ignorance. You are slaves of no one except God, so behave like free men, and never use your freedom as an excuse for wickedness. Have respect for everyone and love for our community; fear God and honour the emperor. (I Peter 2. 13-17)

6. *Wretched Italy, Wicked Florence*

The sheer weight of biblical references in Dante's letter is indicative of the author's deep-seated desire to present Henry, not as a German prince, trying his luck south of the Alps in an attempt to increase his personal power and to expand his area of influence,[49] but as the divinely chosen inheritor of the Roman imperial past, and as a Christ-like figure who will come to cleanse Italy of her (political) sins, and restore her to a state of peace and enlightenment.

Of course, the hopes expressed with such conviction in letter V were already tinged with uncertainty (though by no means completely abandoned) by the time that Dante wrote letters VI and VII some six months later. Nonetheless, both these letters open with the same emphasis on the notion of peace already identified in the opening paragraph of letter V. It is peace that is, for Dante, the main objective of Henry's campaign, and the ability to bring peace to a troubled society which most closely allies Henry with Christ. The continued resistance to Henry on the part of Florence is thus seen not only as an act of political rebellion, but also, in so far as it prevents the attainment of this peace, as an act of rebellion against a greater good, a good willed by God. Letter VI begins, therefore, with a reiteration of Dante's belief that peace and stability in the temporal realm can only be guaranteed by the existence of a universal Emperor: God 'has ordained that human affairs should be governed by the Holy Roman Empire, in order that human beings should enjoy the peace that only the stability of such a government can guarantee, and should live in citizenship with one another throughout the world, in accordance with the will of nature (VI. 1).[50] Dante goes on, however, to state that the necessity of the existence of an emperor for the well-being of the world in general and Italy specifically emerges if one examines the consequences of the absence of such an emperor:

> when the throne of Augustus is vacant, the whole world goes awry, the captain and the oarsmen of the ship of St Peter fall asleep, and wretched Italy, left alone, at the mercy of private decisions and devoid of any public control, is so battered and buffeted by gales and floods

---

[49] Contrast Dante's reference, in *Purgatorio* VI, to 'Alberto tedesco' (*Purg.*, VI. 97). For Dante, the use of 'tedesco' implies a failure, on the part of the Emperor, to understand the true sense of his imperial authority, an acceptance of his merely local role, and an abandonment of his duty towards *all* his (potential) subjects.

[50] This argument had already been put forward not only in letter V, but also in *Convivio*, IV. iv. 4, and would be restated in *Monarchia*, I. v. 9-10.

that words cannot describe it, and the abject Italians themselves can scarcely measure it with their tears. (VI. 1)

This passage bears strong resemblances to the famous invective against Italy in *Purgatorio* VI, which may well also have been composed during the period of Henry's campaign:[51]

> Ahi serva Italia, di dolore ostello,
> nave sanza nocchiere in gran tempesta,
> non donna di province, ma bordello. [...]
>   Cerca, misera, intorno da le prode
> le tue marine, e poi ti guarda in seno,
> s'alcuna parte in te di pace gode.
>   Che val perché ti racconciasse il freno
> Iustinïano, se la sella è vòta?
> Sanz'esso fora la vergogna meno. [...]
>   Vieni a veder la tua Roma che piagne
> vedova e sola, e dí e notte chiama:
> 'Cesare mio, perché non m'accompagne?'.
>   (*Purg.*, VI. 76-78; 85-90; 112-14)

Just as in the 'worst-case scenario' painted in the opening paragraph of the letter to the Florentines, the Italy of the invective is totally devoid of peace; she is 'misera' (wretched), just as in the Latin letter; and, as in the letter, she is deprived of the guidance of the 'captain and oarsmen' who might have steered her to more peaceful waters. The vacant throne of Augustus is echoed in the invective's mention of the 'sella [...] vòta'; and just as the Italy of the letter is 'left alone' and at the mercy of whatever fate may befall her, so in the invective it is Rome – the imperial city itself – which is 'vedova e sola' in the absence of its 'Cesare'. Moreover, this final reference strikingly anticipates the opening words of the letter to the Italian Cardinals (XI), which famously quotes the first

---

[51] Although it is impossible to establish an exact date of composition for the invective, it is very likely that the *Purgatorio* was written at approximately the time of Henry's campaign, and it should not be seen as surprising, therefore, that many similarities can be identified between the 'imperial' letters and aspects of the *Purgatorio*. See Scott, *Political Purgatory*, pp. 48-49 and p. 100.

verse of the book of Lamentations: 'Oh how lonely she sits, the city once thronged with people. She who was great among the nations has become like a widow' (XI. 1; Lamentations 1. 1). In letter XI, as we have seen, it is not the Emperor (or, more precisely, not *only* the Emperor), but the Pope, who has abandoned Rome, leaving her 'widowed', deprived, in fact, of 'both her lights' (XI. 10).

The invective of *Purgatorio* VI also draws a very pessimistic picture of the relationships which characterize even citizens of the same city:

> e ora in te [Italy] non stanno sanza guerra
> li vivi tuoi, e l'un l'altro si rode
> di quei ch'un muro e una fossa serra.
>
> (*Purg.*, VI. 82-84)

This passage, with its emphasis on the verb *rodere*, inevitably recalls Ugolino and Ruggieri, two citizens of Pisa frozen together in the ice of Cocytus;[52] it also, however, reminds the reader of the *Commedia* that Florence too is defined, almost from the beginning of the text, as a 'città partita' (*Inf.*, VI. 61). The letter to the 'most wicked Florentines within the city', too, is predicated on the violence and hatred which taints relationships between citizens of the same city. In this case, though, the groups of citizens who are at one another's throats are not contained within 'a single wall and a single moat'. Rather, it is the voice of the exile which addresses those Florentines who still have their city walls to protect them. Yet the exile too is a citizen, as the *Convivio* makes plain. For, although the city is conventionally identified with those who hold power in it, both those in government and those who oppose the government *are* citizens: 'chiamare solemo la cittade quelli che la tengono e non coloro che la combattono, avvegna che l'uno e l'altro sia cittadino' (*Conv.*, II. vi. 8). In the letter to the Florentines, therefore, Dante speaks both as a fellow-Florentine

---

[52] In *Inferno* XXXIII, Ugolino refers to Ruggieri as the 'traditor ch'i' rodo' (*Inf.*, XXXIII. 8). On the possible reminiscences of the Ugolino episode in *Purgatorio* VI, see Barolini, *Dante's Poets*, pp. 179-84; Honess, 'Dante and Political Poetry', pp. 127-29.

and as an 'undeserving exile',[53] reminding his city of what precisely it stands to lose through its opposition to Henry.

7. Peace on Earth

If the letter to the Princes and Peoples of Italy had expressed Dante's strong conviction that Henry would bring peace and reconciliation to the divided cities of contemporary Italy, while the letter to the Florentines had conveyed the author's sorrow at the continuing lack of peace, in his own city and beyond, then the letter which Dante wrote to Henry himself only eighteen days after composing that to the Florentines seems to sum up both the continued hope for the establishment of a divinely willed imperial peace and his continued disappointment that such a peace seems ever more out of reach. Yet the aspiration towards peace continues to be presented as the prime motivating force in Dante's support for Henry's campaign. Indeed, in the *incipit* to this letter, Dante claims to be speaking not only for himself, but also on behalf of 'all Tuscans who desire peace'. Having established that he is someone for whom the attainment of peace on earth is a key aim, then, Dante begins his letter proper with a reference not to the temporal peace which an Emperor might secure for his subjects, but to the eternal peace of Heaven bequeathed to all Christians by Christ: 'As testimony of the infinite love of God, we have been bequeathed peace, in order that the difficulties of our life as members of the Church Militant on earth might be assuaged by its wonderful sweetness, and that, taking advantage of peace on earth, we might earn the bliss of the Church Triumphant in Heaven' (VII. 1).[54] The same passage from St John's Gospel evoked here is also quoted by Dante in the *Convivio* to illustrate the complete and all-encompassing peace of the Empyrean heaven:

> Lo cielo empireo per la sua pace simiglia la divina scienza, che piena è di tutta pace; la quale non soffera lite alcuna d'oppinioni o di sofistici argomenti, per la

---

[53] This recalls the way in which Dante refers to himself in the 'address line' of all these letters as 'florentinus et exul inmeritus' (a Florentine and an undeserving exile).

[54] 'Peace I bequeath to you, my own peace I give to you, a peace the world cannot give, this is my gift to you' (John 14. 27)

eccellentissima certezza del suo subietto, lo quale è Dio.
E di questa dice esso a li suoi discepoli: 'La pace mia do
a voi, la pace mia lascio a voi'. (*Conv.,* II. xiv. 19)

In the letter, too, perfect peace is associated with Heaven. The peace which Christ bequeaths to Christians on earth may attenuate the difficulties which they face as members of the Church Militant on earth, but can only be fully enjoyed once they attain membership of the Church Triumphant in Heaven.

This is not to say, though, that Dante has abandoned his conviction – seen earlier in relation to letter V – that Henry can not only bring temporal peace to the Church Militant, but also, by doing God's work in carrying out his divinely ordained role, achieve on earth something of the peace enjoyed fully only by the Church Triumphant in Heaven. In the letter to the Princes and Peoples of Italy it was, as we have seen, in particular through the messianic language and biblical references used of Henry throughout, that his peace-bringing mission was presented as an integral part of God's plan for humanity. In fact, such language is also a key feature of the letter to Henry himself. The frustration which Dante feels at Henry's delays and setbacks does not dim his conviction that Henry, and Henry alone, can restore the Empire and bring peace to the world and happiness to the individuals within it. Rather – and paradoxically – the doubts unleashed in Henry's followers by his failure to proceed swiftly to Rome and a triumphant coronation are used by Dante to bind Henry ever more closely to the figure of Christ. Dante maintains that: 'our uncertainty leads us to doubt, and to burst out with the words of Christ's precursor: "Are you the one who is to come, or have we got to wait for someone else?" ' (VII. 2). 'Christ's precursor' is John the Baptist, who – according to the Gospels of Matthew and Luke – sends his followers to Christ from his prison to ask him this very question. Christ's reply to John confirms his messianic status, while exhorting John and his followers to leave their doubts behind and to embrace true faith in him:

> Jesus answered: 'Go back and tell John what you hear
> and see; the blind see again, and the lame walk, lepers are
> cleansed, and the deaf hear, and the dead are raised to life

and the Good News is proclaimed to the poor; and happy
is the man who does not lose faith in me.'[55]

The biblical quotation here enables Dante both to reiterate the Christological role of Henry VII, as set out in the letter of the previous year, and to exhort Henry's doubting followers not to lose faith.

This renewed statement of confidence in Henry is given an even more emphatic expression at the end of this paragraph of the letter, when Dante explains that he has, himself, seen and paid homage to the Emperor-elect:

> For I too, who write this letter both in my own name and on behalf of others, saw in you the great benevolence and heard in you the great humility which are fitting to your imperial majesty, when my hands touched your feet, and my lips paid homage to you. Then my spirit exulted in you, and I silently said to myself: 'Behold the lamb of God that takes away the sins of the world.' (VII. 2)

This statement contains two further confirmations of Henry's Christ-like status. The phrase 'my spirit exulted in you' echoes the words of the *Magnificat*, 'My soul proclaims the greatness of the Lord, and my spirit exults in God my saviour' (Luke 1. 46-47), while the quotation with which the paragraph closes – 'Behold the lamb of God that takes away the sins of the world' – is a reference to the account in St John's Gospel of Christ's acclamation by John the Baptist: 'The next day, seeing Jesus coming towards him, John said, "Look, there is the lamb of God that takes away the sins of the world" ' (John 1. 29). Both these biblical passages recurred as key elements within the liturgy, which would have made them instantly recognizable to Dante's first readers, underlining and also extending their significance. This is particularly true in the case of the *Agnus Dei*, which, in its liturgical formulation, ends with a prayer for peace ('dona nobis pacem'; grant us peace). Interestingly, the *Agnus Dei* also features in *Purgatorio* XVI (the canto of 'Rome's two suns'), and again in the context of a prayer

---

[55] Matthew 11. 2-6; and compare Luke 7. 18-23.

for peace and harmony, the virtues which oppose the sin of Wrath being punished there:[56]

> Io sentia voci, e ciascuna pareva
> pregar per pace e per misericordia
> l'Agnel di Dio che le peccata leva.
> Pur '*Agnus Dei*' eran le loro essordia;
> una parola in tutte era e un modo,
> sí che parea tra esse ogne concordia.
>
> (*Purg.*, XVI. 16-21)

The 'concordia' achieved by the souls who coexist in Purgatory in what seems to be a model of an ideal earthly society,[57] reflects the harmony that Dante believes could be achieved in contemporary Italy (in contrast to the situation of discord described in the invective of canto VI) under a universal Emperor. In the letter, therefore, the earthly peace which Dante hopes to see realized as a result of Henry's mission is compared, once again, to the perfect peace of Heaven, bestowed by the Lamb of God, and this paragraph, with its three unequivocal acclamations of Henry as a Christ-figure, seems to represent the climax of Dante's presentation of Henry from a Christological perspective.

In the closing paragraph of this letter, Dante again portrays Henry VII as having been chosen by God to bring hope and peace to his people. Here, however, the references are to the Old Testament (perhaps taking up the references to Moses and to the Salomonic tradition identified in letter V). Henry is compared, here, not with Christ directly but with David, 'the son of Jesse' (VII. 8), while Florence is identified with David's legendary adversary, Goliath. The identification with David is also, by extension, a further identification with Christ, since (as the opening of St Matthew's Gospel makes clear) Christ is descended from David through his earthly 'father', Joseph,[58] and is born in Bethlehem, the city of David. This reference, moreover, emphasizes the providential view of history which emerges

---

[56] See Barnes, 'Vestiges of the Liturgy', p. 237.

[57] See Honess, *From Florence to the Heavenly City*, pp. 59-63.

[58] See Matthew 1. 1-17.

throughout these letters; for, in the *Convivio*, Dante had already drawn a connection between the history of Israel – and specifically the figure of its great king, David – and the history of Rome:

> E tutto questo fu in uno temporale, che David nacque e nacque Roma, cioè che Enea venne di Troia in Italia, che fu origine de la cittade romana, sì come testimoniano le scritture. Per che assai è manifesto la divina elezione del romano imperio, per lo nascimento de la santa cittade che fu contemporaneo a la radice de la progenie di Maria. (*Conv.*, IV. v. 6)

This connection re-emerges with the birth of Christ in the *plenitudo temporis*, which coincides, for Dante, with the culmination of imperial authority and world peace under Augustus. Letter V had already emphasized this correlation, when it commented that that it was 'after a twelve-year peace which embraced the whole world' that 'the face of the Son of God [...] was revealed, appearing as the culminating point of this process' (V. 9). The providential version of Roman history which Dante presents here goes back at least as far as Orosius:

> So at that time, that is, in that year in which, by the ordination of God, Caesar achieved the strongest and truest peace, Christ was born, upon whose coming this peace waited [...]. Also in this same year, when God deigned to be seen as man and actually to be man, Caesar, whom God had predestined for this great mystery, ordered that a census be taken of each province everywhere and that all men be enrolled. So at that time, Christ was born and was entered on the Roman census list as soon as he was born. [...] It is undoubtedly clear for the understanding of all, from their faith and investigation, that our Lord Jesus Christ brought forward this City to this pinnacle of power, prosperous and protected by His will; of this City, when he came, he especially wished to be called a Roman citizen by the declaration of the Roman census list.[59]

---

[59] Paulus Orosius, *Seven Books of History Against the Pagans*, VI. 22.

Inserting Henry VII into this historical perspective, Dante conflates the figures of Augustus and Christ into the single person of the Emperor-elect. This new Messiah will not come into the world peace created for him by the Emperor, but will himself, through his coming, bring peace to the world, freeing human beings not from their sins *tout court* like Christ, but from the political sins of *cupiditas* and the *libido dominandi* which prevent political stability and impede the individual's progress towards happiness. Letter VII closes with this firm hope – the hope that the inheritance of peace promised to humanity by Christ will be restored by Henry, so that 'as we now sigh in our Babylonian exile when we remember the holy Jerusalem, so then, restored to citizenship and breathing in peace, will we remember in our joy the miseries of our time of confusion' (VII. 8).

8. Babylon and Jerusalem, Florence and Rome

Dante's hopes were, of course, never to come to fruition. Henry was eventually crowned Emperor on 29 June 1312, but without ever having conquered Florence or gained supremacy, and only after a long and humiliating battle to enter Rome itself, resulting in numerous casualties and an intense loss of morale on both sides.[60] With his opponents preventing access to the Vatican, Henry was eventually forced to agree to a coronation in the Basilica of St John Lateran, in a ceremony performed not by the Pope, but by Cardinal Niccolò da Prato. Henry died of malaria in August 1313, almost three years after Dante's announcement that the 'favourable time' had arrived. The despair which Dante must have felt at Henry's failure is not given full expression in any of the poet's works. No letters bear witness to this disappointment; the fictional dating of the *Commedia* in 1300 (long before Henry's election) means that any references to his ill-fated campaign are necessarily vague; and the *Monarchia* is, as we have seen, far more concerned with the theory of imperial rule than with its practice. It is left to the letter to the Italian Cardinals to give the reader a sense of the despondency and hopelessness which characterize Dante's attitude towards the political realities of the post-Henry period.

As has been seen, letter XI opens with another biblical quotation, but it is one which is in direct contrast to the closing

---

[60] See Bowsky, *Henry VII in Italy*, pp. 159-65.

allusion of letter VII, with its hope that Italy's 'Babylonian' exiles will soon weep no more at the memory of their lost Jerusalem.[61] The quotation from the Lamentations of Jeremiah which opens the letter to the Cardinals confirms immediately that the hoped-for renewal has not come about. Dante notes that 'we too, like Jeremiah, find ourselves compelled to weep for our own widowed, lonely city', although, unlike the prophet, who tells of the future destruction of Jerusalem, Dante expresses his grief 'not in anticipation of things to come, but rather in suffering after the event' (XI. 2).

This was, moreover, not the first time that Dante had used Jeremiah's words to evoke a tragedy that had already occurred. As the reader of his earlier works would doubtless have recalled, he had already compared himself to Jeremiah in another letter, a letter which – if indeed it was ever actually written – has not survived. In the *Vita nuova*, Dante marks the death of Beatrice by quoting this same biblical verse (*VN*, XXVIII. 1); and later he explains that, in the absence of Beatrice 'rimase tutta la sopradetta cittade quasi vedova dispogliata da ogni dignitade; onde io, ancora lagrimando in questa desolata cittade, scrissi a li principi de la terra alquanto de la sua condizione, pigliando quello cominciamento di Geremia profeta che dice: '*Quomodo sedet sola civitas*' (*VN*, XXX. 1). The lonely, widowed Rome of letter XI, therefore, recalls not only Jerusalem, but also the lonely, widowed city of Florence, deprived not of her political lights, but of the divine presence of Beatrice.

To the reader of Dante's political letters, this reminder of the fact that Florence, too, had once been lamented by Dante as a second Jerusalem, only serves to emphasize how far his home town had fallen in the little more than twenty years since the death of Beatrice. It has fallen so far, in fact, that, far from being identified with Jerusalem, by 1311 Dante is able to compare it with the city which traditionally opposes Jerusalem: Babylon. This comparison is made explicitly in the letter to the Florentines themselves. Why – Dante asks – 'do you insist on forsaking the holy Empire and on trying to build new kingdoms, like second Babylonians, as if the politics of Florence were one thing and that of Rome something quite different?' (VI. 2). The image here is an image of presumption, the presumption which, we have seen, lies at the root

---

[61] The reference is to Psalm 136 [137]. 1: 'Beside the streams of Babylon we sat and wept at the memory of Zion.'

of the *libido dominandi* and of political and social unrest, and characterizes St Augustine's 'City of Man'. And indeed while, for Augustine, the 'City of God' can be identified, on a spiritual level, with Jerusalem, the 'City of Man' is represented by Babylon: 'The name Sion means "contemplation"; for she contemplates the great blessing of the age to come, since all her striving is directed to that end. She is also Jerusalem, in the same spiritual sense [...]. Her enemy is Babylon, the city of the Devil, whose name means "confusion" '.[62] Moreover, Babylon is traditionally conflated with Babel, the first rebellious city of the Bible, which was also understood etymologically as 'confusion'.[63]

In her resistance to Henry VII, Florence presumes to claim the right to self-government, setting herself up as a separate authority, equal, not subject, to the Emperor, another moon in the sky. In this, she is like the builders of Babel, whose tower rises towards the heavens in a direct challenge to the authority of God himself,[64] and for this, in Dante's eyes, she deserves to be punished, to be literally 'confounded', just like her biblical antecedent. Like Nimrod and his followers, the Florentines construct the towers which, in their arrogance, they believe will allow them to determine their own destiny, and Dante predicts that, as in the case of Nimrod, their presumption will end only in defeat as their towers come tumbling down: 'you will see the buildings, which you did not erect prudently according to your needs, but rather developed recklessly for your own pleasure, destroyed by battering-rams and burned by

---

[62] *City of God*, XVII. 16. Ferrante also comments on Dante's likening of Rome to Jerusalem and Florence to Babylon, but links these two opposing cities specifically with Heaven and Hell respectively as models for the realms described in the *Paradiso* and the *Inferno*. 'Because he is concerned with the contemporary situation in Italy, Dante shifts from the traditional types for heaven and hell – Jerusalem and Babylon – to the more immediate counterparts, Rome and Florence' (*Political Vision*, p. 48).

[63] 'Yahweh scattered them thence over the whole face of the earth, and they stopped building the town. It was named Babel therefore, because there Yahweh confused the language of the whole earth' (Genesis 11. 8-9).

[64] ' "Come" they said "let us build ourselves a town and a tower with its top reaching heaven. Let us make a name for ourselves, so that we may not be scattered about the whole earth" ' (Genesis 11. 4). Dante's retelling of the Babel story in the *De vulgari eloquentia* makes the political dimension of this sin very clear, as I have argued in *From Florence to the Heavenly City*, pp. 152-53. See also Keen, *Dante and the City*, p. 101.

fire' (VI. 4). This criticism of Florence's arrogance seems to prefigure Cacciaguida's attack, in *Paradiso* XV, on the grotesque over-confidence of the city's attempt to out-do Rome, not only by challenging its political authority, but also in purely architectural terms. Cacciaguida contrasts the building of vast and luxurious houses with the simple, frugal life which he himself had known in the city two centuries earlier, and he too makes a prediction that – as at Babel – pride will come before a fall, so that where Florence has become even more spectacular than Rome, so her decline will also outdo that of the city to which she ought to look with the respect which a daughter owes her mother:[65]

> Non avea case di famiglia vòte;
> non v'era giunto ancor Sardanapalo
> a mostrar ciò che 'n camere si puote.
> Non era vinto ancora Montemalo
> dal vostro Uccellatoio, che, com'è vinto
> nel montar sú, cosí sarà nel calo.
>
> (*Par.*, XV. 106-10)

In view of this parallel, it is perhaps not surprising that, in *Paradiso* XVI, Cacciaguida goes on to identify the 'principio [...] del mal de la cittade' as 'la *confusion* de le persone' (*Par.*, XVI. 67-68; my italics). By identifying Florence as a city characterized by 'confusion', Cacciaguida is implicitly lending the weight of his heavenly perspective to the view of his home town which Dante had already put forward in his letter to the 'wicked Florentines within the city'.

Dante's prophecy of the future ruin of Florence in letter VI goes on to predict that the sins of the Florentine fathers will be visited upon their 'bewildered and ignorant' children (VI. 4). This notion also finds an echo in the *Paradiso* in a context which again brings together Florence, Rome and Jerusalem. 'Molte fiate già pianser li figli | per la colpa del padre' (*Par.*, VI. 109-10), states Justinian at the end of his long account of the history of the Roman Eagle; and here, like Dante in letter VI, it would seem that the Emperor is specifically thinking of Florence as he attacks both Guelphs and

---

[65] In the *Convivio*, Florence is described as the 'bellissima e famosissima figlia di Roma' (*Conv.*, I. iii. 4).

Ghibellines for, on the one hand, their opposition to imperial authority and, on the other, their appropriation of the imperial emblem as a party-political, rather than a universal, symbol,[66] leading to the factionalism which divides citizens one against the other. Yet there is a broader context here too, which perhaps serves to cast further light on Dante's judgement on Florence in his letter. Only a few lines before he turns to criticize the Guelphs and Ghibellines, Justinian has described how the imperial eagle 'con Tito a far vendetta corse | de la vendetta del peccato antico' (*Par.*, VI. 92-93); that is, how Rome, acting as the agent of divine judgement, had avenged the death of Christ by destroying Jerusalem in AD 70. Justinian's reference to Jerusalem's devastation by Titus cannot help but call to mind once again the voice of Jeremiah, lamenting the earlier destruction of his own Jerusalem. And, indeed, Jeremiah too suggests that this destruction can be attributed to the sins of the fathers being visited on their sons, when he writes: 'Our fathers have sinned; they are no more, and we ourselves bear the weight of their crimes' (Lamentations 5. 7).

There is an obvious paradox here, in that Dante seems to be suggesting, in the letter which he addresses to the city's leaders, that Florence can be compared both to Babylon/Babel and to Jerusalem. This paradox is only apparent, however, since Jerusalem, in the Judaeo-Christian tradition, had never been an incontrovertibly positive symbol, despite its recurrent use as a symbol for Heaven. This can be seen both in the books of the Prophets, where the city is alternately praised as God's chosen city and condemned as the sinful city which ignores God's commandments and brings disaster down on itself,[67] and in the Gospels, where Jerusalem is presented primarily as a place of

---

[66] 'L'uno al pubblico segno i gigli gialli | oppone, e l'altro appropria quello a parte, | sí ch'è forte a veder chi piú si falli' (*Par.*, VI. 100-02).

[67] Ezekiel, for example, addresses Jerusalem as follows: 'City [...], you have incurred guilt by the blood you have shed, you have defiled yourself with the idols you have made, you have brought your hour closer, you have come to the end of your time. And so I have made you an object of scorn to the nations and a laughing-stock to every country' (Ezekiel 22. 3-4). The prophets also very frequently compare Jerusalem to the wicked cities *par excellence*, Sodom and Gomorrah (see, for example, Isaiah 1. 10; Isaiah 3. 9; Jeremiah 23. 14) and to a prostitute (see, for example, Isaiah 1. 21; Jeremiah 13. 26-27; Ezekiel 23. 2-3). See also Honess, *From Florence to the Heavenly City*, pp. 139-43.

opposition to Christ's ministry and as the site of the Crucifixion.[68] Indeed, the prediction of Florence's downfall in paragraph 4 of letter VI has many parallels with Christ's own lament for the presumptuous blindness of Jerusalem which follows his triumphal entry into the city:

> Yes, a time is coming when your enemies will raise fortifications all round you, when they will encircle you and hem you in on every side; they will dash you and the children inside your walls to the ground; they will leave not one stone standing on another within you – and all because you did not recognise your opportunity when God offered it![69]

From this perspective, then, the implicit parallel between Florence and Jerusalem hinted at by Justinian takes on a far greater significance within Dante's political letters. For if – as we have seen – the letters compare Henry himself consistently and repeatedly with Christ, then it does not require a huge effort of the imagination to view Florence herself in the guise of the rebellious Jerusalem, which rejects Christ and puts him to death on the Cross.

9. 'A Voice Crying in the Wilderness'

Moreover, a closer reading of these letters with this comparison in mind, also reveals implications for our understanding of the role and status of Dante himself. In letter VII, in particular, the Christological references which Dante attaches to Henry are specifically connected to the figure of John the Baptist and his recognition of Christ as the Messiah,[70] in a way which suggests that, if Henry is a new Messiah, then Dante himself, who announces his coming, is a new John, a 'voice crying in the wilderness', announcing the coming of the Emperor.[71] Indeed, Dante tells us that he had silently repeated to himself John's acclamation – 'Behold the lamb of God that takes away the sins of the world' – when he had seen and paid homage to the Emperor in

---

[68] See Dougherty, *The Fivesquare City*, p. 15.

[69] Luke 19. 43-44. See Martinez, 'Dante's Jeremiads', p. 302. Martinez also points out that these parallels are not limited to the biblical text, but are also found in a long tradition of Fall of Jerusalem narratives.

person, confirming his symbolic acceptance of the role of the Baptist. And this identification, of course, takes on renewed political significance in the light of the fact that John the Baptist was also the patron saint of Florence. Dante seems to be suggesting that he alone – an exile and an outsider, like John himself – is the bearer of Florence's authentic voice.

This comparison is more fitting than might, perhaps, at first appear. Dante is exiled against his will from his beloved Florence, rather than freely choosing the life of an outsider, yet he clearly does see himself in the early years of his exile as a wilderness-dweller of sorts:

> Poi che fu piacere de li cittadini de la bellissima e famosissima figlia di Roma, Fiorenza, di gittarmi fuori del suo dolce seno [...], per le parti quasi tutte a le quali questa lingua si stende, peregrino, quasi mendicando, sono andato [...]. Veramente, io sono stato legno sanza vela e sanza governo, portato a diversi porti e foci e liti dal vento secco che vapora la dolorosa povertade. (*Conv.*, I. iii. 5)

And, like John,[72] he also takes on the voice of a prophet. The whole of paragraph 4 of letter VI is avowedly prophetic, as Dante predicts the final downfall of Florence, which he claims (ironically, in view

---

[70] See above. The biblical passages referred to are at Matthew 11. 2-3, Luke 7. 18-23, and John 1. 29.

[71] 'It is written in the book of the prophet Isaiah: *Look, I am going to send my messenger before you; he will prepare your way. A voice cries in the wilderness: prepare a way for the Lord, make his paths straight*, and so it was that John the Baptist appeared in the wilderness, proclaiming a baptism of repentance for the forgiveness of sins' (Mark 1. 2-4). See also Matthew 3. 3; Luke 3. 4; John 1. 23; and compare Isaiah 40. 3. This identification is also noted by Mineo in *Profetismo e apocalittica*, p. 149.

[72] 'Jesus began to talk to the people about John: "What did you go into the wilderness to see? A reed swaying in the breeze? No? Then what did you go out to see? A man wearing fine clothes? Oh no, those who wear fine clothes are to be found in palaces. Then what did you go out for? To see a prophet? Yes, I tell you, and much more than a prophet' (Matthew 11. 7-9). Indeed, medieval interpretations of this passage suggested that John was 'more than a prophet' or the greatest of the prophets precisely because he had seen Christ with his own eyes, just as Dante emphasizes in letter VII that he has personally seen and paid homage to Henry VII (see Mineo, *Profetismo e apocalittica*, p. 150).

of Henry's ultimate failure to conquer the city) has been revealed 'both by unequivocal signs and by unquestionable arguments', and in the later letters this prophetic role is confirmed as Dante aligns himself first with John the Baptist (letter VII) and then with Jeremiah (letter XI).[73]

Raffaello Morghen identifies the writing of letter XI as marking a turning-point in Dante's development, and sees the letter as proving that 'in un certo momento, Dante ebbe la coscienza di aver quasi avuto dall'alto l'autorità di parlare ai grandi della terra e a tutto il popolo cristiano col tono ammonitore del profeta' ('Dante profeta', p. 152), although, as we have seen, this prophetic tone also characterizes letters V, VI, and VII.[74] In fact, the real turning-point for Dante, the moment at which his voice begins to speak out not merely as a representative of a political party or faction, but with the authority of a mouthpiece for divine truths ('consapevole portatore del monito di Dio'; Morghen, 'Dante profeta', p. 152), seems to come between the writing of letter I on behalf of the exiled Florentine Whites in 1304 and Henry's election in 1309.[75]

10. Political Letters, 'Poema sacro'

Soon after Dante must have written to Niccolò da Prato, the 'peace-maker' left Florence with her factional strife raging as strongly as ever; within less than a month Pope Benedict XI was also dead, and with him the political will to resolve the city's factional differences. Dante soon distanced himself from the group of White exiles on behalf of whom he had written his first letter, and became, as *Paradiso* XVII memorably has it, a 'parte per [se] stesso'. This separation and isolation is not construed by Dante, however, as a negative thing, a confirmation and intensification of the sense of solitariness and rejection brought about by his exile (as

---

[73] A second prophetic point of contact in letter XI is Ezekiel, referred to in paragraph 4, who, according to Di Scipio, is 'the most appropriate source and exemplum for Dante's own prophetic utterances', due to his 'unique [...] interest in the temple and the liturgy' (*Pauline Thought*, p. 174).

[74] Mineo talks of the 'carattere profeticamente ispirato' ('Mondo classico e città terrena', p. 71) of the letters written at the time of Henry VII's campaign.

[75] Bruno Nardi also identifies this period with Dante's assumption of a 'prophetic' voice ('Dante profeta', p. 339).

expressed, for example, in the quotation from *Convivio* I. iii, above). Rather, Cacciaguida makes clear that his rejection of factionalism and party politics will be a positive thing: 'a te fia bello | averti fatto parte per te *stesso* (*Par.*, XVII. 68-69; my italics). Dante's isolation is, as Brunetto recognizes in his prophecy of the poet's exile in *Inferno* XV, a direct consequence of his virtues, which differentiate him from his fellow citizens: 'ché tra li lazzi sorbi | si disconvien fruttar al dolce fico' (*Inf.*, XV. 65-66). In the wicked Florence, Brunetto implies, the virtuous Dante was already an outsider, and his exile is merely the confirmation of a pre-existing moral condition.[76] His deliberate choice, sometime after 1304, to speak with the voice of the outsider reveals his acceptance of this fact and his decision to exploit it as a platform for the moral, religious, and political truths which he expresses in the *Commedia* and the political letters.

As Giuseppe Mazzotta has convincingly argued, Dante's exile and the prophetic tone which he adopts thereafter are inextricably bound up together:

> Exile is the condition from which his voice rises, but the displacement does not entail a complacent isolation within a world largely indifferent to the private truth the poet witnesses. [...] Like the prophets, Dante makes of exile a virtue and a necessary perspective from which to speak to the world and from which he can challenge its expectations and assumptions; like the prophets, he also acknowledges that the truth he communicates is, paradoxically, what further alienates him from the world he has already lost. (*Dante's Vision*, p. 179)

Dante's becoming a 'party of one' gives him the necessary distance to challenge all those (irrespective of party) who would oppose his political ideal, while at the same time his fearlessness in speaking out against what he sees as the wrongs (political and otherwise) of his own time only helps to confirm his status as an outsider.[77] As he adopts more and more frequently and with increasing conviction the voice of the prophet, who will inevitably be rejected in his own country,[78] Dante comes to accept his exile as the necessary and

---

[76] See Honess, *From Florence to the Heavenly City*, pp. 29-31.

inevitable consequence of his willingness to speak out as 'a lone voice of devotion' (XI. 6), so that, as Cacciaguida tells him, in language that has itself been defined as 'prophetic' in tone:[79]

> Questo tuo grido farà come vento,
> che le piú alte cime piú percuote;
> e ciò non fa d'onor poco argomento.
> <div align="right">(<i>Par.</i>, XVII. 133-35)</div>

The result is his divinely inspired and prophetic 'poema sacro | al quale ha posto mano e cielo e terra' (*Par.*, XXV. 1-2).

Dante's political letters, like the *Commedia*, represent an authentic expression of this desire to speak the truth ('[rimuovere] ogne menzogna') and to let his 'parola brusca' be heard, leaving those who are made to feel uncomfortable by his pronouncements to 'grattar dov'è la rogna' (*Par.*, XVII. 126-29). Far from being the dry political tracts which they are sometimes supposed to be, they are – as I hope to have shown in this introduction – deeply passionate texts, dealing – yes – with politics, but with politics on a grand scale, with politics in the sense in which it affects all human beings in their quest for the 'vita felice' (*Conv.*, IV. iv. 1). As such, their inspiration and rhetoric are closely bound up with those of the *Commedia*, as they too speak out with unshakeable conviction and fearless directness 'in pro del mondo che mal vive' (*Purg.*, XXXII. 103).

---

[77] 'Come i profeti biblici parlano in nome di una diretta rivelazione di Dio e rappresentano l'ispirazione individuale, la quale, pur traendo alimento dalla vita religiosa di tutto un popolo, si afferma all'infuori dell'istituto sacerdotale e talora in contrasto con esso, allo stesso modo Dante, laico, fatto ardito dalla visione concessagli per singolare grazia divina, non teme di denunciare nella mala condotta dei pastori della chiesa la cagione che il mondo ha fatto reo e di scagliare contro di essi le sue amare invettive' (Nardi, 'Dante profeta', p. 408). And the point which Nardi makes here in relation to religious authorities is equally true of Dante's attitude towards secular authorities in both the letters and the *Commedia*.

[78] 'I tell you solemnly, no prophet is ever accepted in his own country' (Luke 4. 24); compare Matthew 13. 57; Mark 6. 4; John 4. 44.

[79] See, for example, Schnapp, *The Transfiguration of History*, pp. 236-37.

Dante Alighieri: Four Political Letters

The Letter to the Princes and Peoples of Italy (Letter V)

Introduction: Autumn 1310

Henry, Count of Luxembourg, was elected King of the Romans and Emperor-elect on 27 November 1308 and crowned by the Archbishop of Cologne in Aachen on 6 January 1309. Almost immediately, he began to plan what he hoped would be a triumphal journey to Italy, in order to be crowned as Empire in Rome. In July 1309, he sent messengers to Italy with copies of a royal encyclical in which Henry expressed his hopes of bringing peace to the peninsula. In the same month Henry's election was recognized by Pope Clement V in the encyclical *Divinae Sapientiae*, in return for which Henry's ambassadors swore in his name that he would defend the Church and not attempt to usurp papal authority in Rome and the Papal States.

In spring 1310, Henry sent legations to visit the states of Tuscany and Lombardy, charged with preparing the way for his forthcoming expedition. In Lombardy the legates were greeted with enthusiasm – in those cities which were nominally Guelph as well as in those which claimed a Ghibelline allegiance. In Tuscany, however, the situation was very different. Although Pisa (traditionally Florence's fiercest opponent in the region) welcomed the legates, Florence and her allies refused to acknowledge Henry's jurisdiction over their territories and agreed to support the Emperor-elect with cash and troops only in return for his renunciation of any claim to exercise authority over these lands.

Indications of potential resistance in Tuscany were not strong enough, however, to dampen Henry's enthusiasm for his Italian campaign and his confidence in its success. In August 1310, Henry promised Clement V that he would not attempt to infringe upon the rights and jurisdictions of the Italian Guelphs. In return, Clement issued the encyclical *Exultet in Gloria* of 1 September 1310, in which he ordered all cities and prelates subject to the Emperor to receive Henry as their temporal lord. This encyclical seemed to give Henry the final confirmation that he needed, and on 13 September he issued an encyclical of his own announcing his imminent departure for Italy.

Henry crossed the Alps with his army, and arrived in Italy – in the small commune of Susa – on 23 October 1310. After resting for six days, he proceeded to Turin and thence to Chieri, to Asti, and finally to Milan, where he arrived on 11 December. In all these towns Henry received oaths of loyalty from the citizens and attempted to establish new and peaceful regimes though the restoration of exiles and the appointment of an imperial vicar.[1]

The exact date of Dante's letter to the Princes and Peoples of Italy is not known. It was undoubtedly written after 1 September, since it makes clear reference, in paragraph 10, to the encyclical *Exultet in Gloria*, and it is widely believed to have been written in September or October 1310, in the very early days of Henry's mission.[2] It expresses the fervent hope that Clement's encyclical will be followed to the letter by Henry's subjects in Italy, who are exhorted to 'hasten before him and declare [their] obedience to him' (V, 4). More than this, though, Dante implores his readers to accept Henry as their political saviour and to see his advent as a new beginning for war-torn Italy, which he hopes to see restored to peace and harmony through the establishment of a new universal political order.

---

[1] For the historical background to Henry's election and the preparations for his campaign, see Bowsky, *Henry VII in Italy*, pp. 19-49; for Henry's early weeks in Italy, see pp. 54-72.

[2] See Toynbee, *Epistolae*, pp. 44-45.

Letter V

Letter V

To each and every one of the Kings of Italy, and to the Senators of the Holy City,[1] and also to Italy's Dukes, Marquises, and Counts, and to her people, a humble Italian, Dante Alighieri, a Florentine undeservedly in exile, prays for peace.

[1] 'Now is the favourable time',[2] when signs of solace and of peace are emerging. For a new day is breaking and the light of that dawn is now allaying the shadows of our long period of adversity. Now the East winds are increasing. The sky is glowing red to its farthest reaches and its gentle calm is inspiring hope in all people. And we too, who for so long have endured the dark night of the wilderness, shall see our long-awaited source of joy, when Titan[3] will rise in peace, and when Justice – which has become dim, like the heliotrope,[4] in the sun's absence – will be revived by the touch of the first light of day. All those who hunger and thirst for justice

---

[1] Note that for Dante the 'Holy City' is always and exclusively Rome (and not, as might perhaps be expected, that other Christian 'holy city', Jerusalem). Compare *Convivio*, IV. v (where the designation 'santa cittade' appears in §§ 6 and 20) and *Monarchia*, II. iv. 5 (where Rome is 'God's chosen city').

[2] II Corinthians 6. 2. The passage in II Corinthians ('For he says: *At the favourable time I have listened to you; on the day of salvation I came to your help.* Well, now is the favourable time; this is the day of salvation') quotes a passage from Isaiah which equally predicts a coming time of peace, when prisoners (and perhaps also those 'undeservedly in exile') will be free once again: 'Thus says Yahweh: At the favourable time I will answer you, on the day of salvation I will help you. [...] I will restore your land and assign you the estates that lie waste. I will say to the prisoners, "Come out", to those who are in darkness, "Show yourselves"' (Isaiah 49. 8-9). In both biblical passages the certainty of God's imminent intervention to restore order to human affairs is clear.

[3] 'Titan' here indicates the sun. Henry VII is also compared to Titan in letter VII. 1.

[4] 'Heliotrope' comes from a Greek word, literally meaning 'turning towards the sun'. Some commentators suggest that this refers to one of a number of flowers of the genus *heliotropium* which turn their flowers and leaves towards the sun. Others (more persuasively in this context) suggest a gemstone, also known as bloodstone, whose red spots were thought either to turn sunlight red as they reflected it or to darken and lighten under the sun's rays. It is probably this latter effect that is intended here. Dante refers to the heliotrope's supposed power to render its carrier invisible in *Inferno*, XXIV. 93, and this is humorously taken up by Boccaccio in day VIII, story 3 of the *Decameron*.

will then be satisfied in the light of his radiance,[5] while those who love injustice will be confounded by his dazzling face. For the great Lion of the tribe of Judah has pricked up his merciful ears,[6] and, taking pity on the lamentations of our universal captivity, he has called up a new Moses, who will deliver his people from their Egyptian oppression and lead them to a land flowing with milk and honey.[7]

[2] Now is the time for you to rejoice, Italy. You, whom now even the Saracens should pity,[8] will soon be envied the whole world over, because your bridegroom, the world's comforter and glory of your people,[9] that most merciful Henry, holy Augustus and Caesar,[10] is hurrying to his wedding.[11] Dry your tears, most beautiful one, and remove all trace of your grief, for he who will

---

[5] Compare Matthew 5. 6: 'Happy those who hunger and thirst for what is right; they shall be satisfied'.

[6] The 'Lion of Judah' is a biblical term used to designate the Messiah, as for example in Genesis 49. 9-10: 'Judah is a lion cub [...] The sceptre shall not pass from Judah, nor the mace from between his feet, until he come to whom it belongs, to whom the people shall render obedience.' The term was also associated with King David, and recurs in the book of Revelation, where it is 'the Lion of the tribe of Judah, the Root of David' which opens the scroll sealed with seven seals (Revelation 5. 5). This is the first of many instances of messianic imagery being attached to Henry VII in these letters.

[7] The land of milk and honey is, of course, a reference to the Promised Land (see, for example, Deuteronomy 6. 3); but the implication here is that, whereas Moses leads his people out of Egypt and to the Promised Land, Henry VII will make of Italy itself a new 'Promised Land'.

[8] See letter XI. 10: 'Rome [...] whom now Hannibal himself [...] should pity.'

[9] The identification of Henry with Christ is emphasized once again through this echo of the *Nunc dimittis*: 'my eyes have seen the salvation which you have prepared for all the nations to see, a light to enlighten the pagans and the glory of your people Israel' (Luke 2. 30-32). Moreover, the image of Henry as a bridegroom recalls the language of the Song of Songs, exegesis of which most often identified the bridegroom with Christ and the Bride with the Church.

[10] The term *divus* ('holy') was used in the Classical period to refer to those Roman emperors who were deified after their deaths.

[11] Henry is described as being called to partake in a different nuptial feast in *Paradiso* XXX, where Beatrice tells Dante that ' 'n quel gran seggio a che tu li occhi tieni | [...] | prima che tu a queste nozze ceni | sederà l'alma [...] | de l'alto Arrigo' (*Par.*, XXX. 133-37). Here the celebration is not of the union of Henry with Italy (whom he will attempt to 'drizzare [...] | [...] in prima ch'ella sia disposta' (*Par.*, XXX. 137-38)), but of his union with God.

free you from the prison of the ungodly is nearby. Striking at the wicked with the edge of his sword,[12] he will destroy them, and will entrust his vineyard to other tenants who will repay him at harvest-time with the fruits of justice.[13]

[3] But will he really take pity on noone? On the contrary, he will forgive anyone who begs for mercy, for he is Caesar and his majesty flows from the Fountainhead of Pity.[14] His judgement abhors vindictiveness, and whereas he always falls short of the mean in meting out punishment, he goes beyond it when it comes to rewarding. So will he then cheer the audacity of the wicked, and drink a toast to the enterprises of the presumptuous? Heaven forbid! For he is the Emperor; and, as Emperor, is it not only right that he should punish the crimes of those who have fallen back into sin, and pursue them until they are utterly defeated, just as Caesar finally defeated Pompey at Thessaly?[15]

---

[12] The phrase 'with the edge of his sword' is a biblical one, used frequently in the Old Testament. See Numbers 21. 24 ('Israel struck him down with the edge of the sword'), and compare, for example, Joshua 10. 28-39.

[13] This sentence recalls the parable of the wicked husbandmen, in which a landowner leases his vineyard to tenants while he is abroad. When the time comes for the harvest the landowner sends his servants to the tenants to collect the produce, but the tenants beat and kill the servants, and later also kill the landowner's son, in an attempt to keep the harvest for themselves. Jesus then asks: 'Now when the owner of the vineyard comes, what will he do to those tenants?' and the Pharisees reply 'He will bring those wretches to a wicked end and lease the vineyard to other tenants who will deliver the produce to him when the season arrives' (Matthew 21. 33-41).

[14] Compare *Monarchia*, II. v. 5: 'Thus with good reason was it written: "The Roman Empire is born of the fountainhead of piety".' The Latin *pietas* (like the Italian *pietà*) can mean both 'pity' and 'piety', although 'pity' is clearly the more appropriate translation in the present context. The phrase seems to be a medieval commonplace, frequently used by the Imperial Chancellery in its communications. The 'fountain of pity' may also be Christ, as in the concluding canzone of Petrarch's *Canzoniere*, addressed to the Virgin Mary: 'tu partoristi il fonte di pietate' (366; line 43), once again underlining the Christological associations of Henry.

[15] The original Latin literally reads: '... and pursue them as far as Thessaly, the Thessaly of the final defeat'. The defeat referred to, though, is clearly that of Pompey at the hands of Julius Caesar at the Battle of Pharsalus, in Thessaly (Northern Greece), in 48 BC. At the same time as being compared with Christ, Henry VII is therefore also being aligned with the great victories of the Roman Empire of the past.

[4] Give up the savage ways you have adopted, you descendants of the Lombards; and if anything should remain of the seed of the Trojans and the Romans,[16] yield to it, so that, when the heavenly eagle comes, descending like lightning,[17] he does not see his own chicks cast out and the rightful place of his offspring occupied by ravens. Come now, you Scandinavian race,[18] and make yourselves eager to receive, as is your duty, [19] the one whose arrival you justifiably fear. Do not let yourselves be seduced by the ploys of cupidity,[20] which, like the Sirens, uses its charm to overcome the

---

[16] This passage is very reminiscent of the attack of the soul of Brunetto Latini, in *Inferno* XV, on the equally 'barbarous' Fiesolans: 'Faccian le bestie fiesolane strame | di lor medesme, e non tocchin la pianta, | s'alcun surge ancora in lor letame, | in cui riviva la sementa santa | di que' Roman che vi rimaser quando | fu fatto il nido di malizia tanta' (*Inf.*, XV. 73-78). See also *Inferno*, XXVI. 60, where the Trojans are identified as the 'gentil seme' of the Romans.

[17] Note the echo of Dante-Pilgrim's dream in *Purgatorio* IX, in which he sees 'un'aguglia [...] con penne d'oro': 'Poi mi parea che [...] | terribil come folgor discendesse' (*Purg.*, IX. 20; 28-29). Although the eagle of the dream is explicitly identified with the disguise adopted by Jupiter in order to snatch Ganymede, it cannot but recall implicitly also the imperial symbol.

[18] The legendary Scandinavian origins of the Lombards is recorded by Paul the Deacon, who states that 'the race of Winnili, that is, of Langobards, which afterwards ruled prosperously in Italy, deducing its origin from the German peoples, came from the island which is called Scadinavia [sic]' (*History of the Lombards*, I. 1).

[19] Both Toynbee and Hardie interpret the phrase 'quod ex vobis est' as 'in so far as you are able'. Frugoni, however, translates the phrase, more plausibly, as 'perché dipende da voi', and this meaning is reflected here. Hence, the success of Henry's mission depends on the Italians, the rightful heirs of the Romans and Trojans, whose duty it is to give the Emperor-elect the support he needs.

[20] The notion of *cupiditas* is vital to an understanding of Dante's political thought. In *Convivio*, IV. iv. 3, he famously explains that 'l'animo umano in terminata possessione di terra non si queti, ma sempre desideri gloria d'acquistare', leading to a state of constant conflict at all levels of the political order, conflict which can only be resolved by the presence of a Universal Emperor, who, by virtue of his very universality, can prevent the destabilizing effects of cupidity in the smaller communities under his jurisdiction. The same view is put forward in *Monarchia*, I. xiii. 7: 'Therefore, since the monarch can have no occasion for greed [...] and since it is greed alone which perverts judgment and obstructs justice, it follows that he alone [...] can be well disposed to rule.' Although often translated as 'greed' or 'avarice' (as in the passage from *Monarchia* just cited), the notion of *cupiditas* does not only involve avarice in the sense of an excessive desire for possessions, but extends also to immoderate desires in general, including excessive ambition.

vigilance of reason.[21] Hasten before him and declare your obedience to him; rejoice in singing a psalm of penitence to him, bearing in mind that 'anyone who resists authority is rebelling against God's decision',[22] while anyone who rebels against God's decisions is kicking out against an omnipotent will, and 'it is hard to kick against the goad'.[23]

[5] You, on the other hand, who lament in your oppression, lift up your hearts, for your salvation is near.[24] Take up the hoe of true humility and break up the arid clods of wrath, level out the field of your mind in case the heavenly rains should happen to come before your seed is sown and so fall from on high in vain. Do not let God's grace be turned away from you, as the stones deflect the morning dew, but be like a fertile valley where lush vegetation – the vegetation which bears true peace as its fruit – germinates and puts out shoots, so that when the green colour of spring comes to your land, the new tenant of Rome will yoke the oxen of his judgement to the plough with greater love and with greater trust. Exercise restraint from now on, my beloved ones, you who, like me, have suffered injustice, so that the Trojan shepherd might

---

[21] This is reminiscent of Dante-Pilgrim's second dream in *Purgatorio*, in which he dreams of a hideous, deformed hag, who is transformed by his gaze into a beautiful woman, who sings: 'Io sono [...] io son dolce serena, | che ' marinari in mezzo mar dismaga' (*Purg.*, XIX. 19-20). Virgil later explains that the Siren of the dream represents the way in which human desires can overwhelm the faculty of reason.

[22] Romans 13. 2. In this passage as a whole, Paul urges the early Church in Rome to respect and obey civil authority: 'Since all government comes from God, the civil authorities were appointed by God, and so anyone who resists authority is rebelling against God's decision, and such an act is bound to be punished. [...] The state is there to serve God for your benefit'.

[23] See Acts 26. 14 (also, in some Bible translations, Acts 9. 5), where the phrase refers to St Paul's futile persecution of Christians. The phrase is a Greek proverbial expression for futile resistance, and comes from the traditional way of driving oxen, using a long stick with a point on one end. If an ox resisted the goad by kicking out against it, the point would simply be driven further into the animal's flesh, increasing its pain. The wording used here does not exactly follow that of the Jerusalem Bible in order to make better sense of Dante's passage.

[24] Compare Luke 21. 28: 'And then they will see the Son of Man coming in a cloud with power and great glory. When these things begin to take place, stand erect, hold your heads high, because your liberation is near at hand.' This reference reinforces once again the identification of Henry VII with the Messiah.

recognize you as sheep from his own sheepfold.[25] For, although divine providence has entrusted him with the exercise of earthly punishment, and although he does take pleasure in correcting his family, nonetheless he derives even greater pleasure from showing it compassion, in order that he may stand as an image of the goodness of God, the single point from which the powers of Peter and of Caesar both emerge.[26]

[6] If, therefore, you do not allow yourselves to be held back by that first sin which very often bends over backwards like a snake and turns on itself,[27] it should now be clear to you all[28] that peace is being prepared for each and every one of you, and you should already be able to enjoy a foretaste of unhoped-for happiness. Wake up therefore, all of you; rise up to meet your king, you

---

[25] In the Latin, the ideal Trojan lineage of Henry VII is indicated through the adjective 'Hectoreus', a reference to Hector, the bravest of the Trojans, who was killed by Achilles.

[26] See *Monarchia*, III. xii, in which Dante refutes the claims of those who argue that 'all things belonging to a single species are referred to one thing which is the measure for all things which belong to that species; but all men belong to the same species; therefore they are to be referred to one man as their common measure. [...] And since the pope must not be referred to any other man, it remains that the emperor along with all other men must be referred to him'. Dante explains that, while it is true that *in terms of their humanity* all human beings can be related to one another, the pope and the emperor *in terms of their office* exercise quite different functions and thus cannot be viewed as belonging to a 'single species'. And since both papal and imperial offices are defined as 'relationships of authority' they must be referred to the supreme principle of authority, that is, to God, 'in whom all principles form an absolute unity'. Thus here God is defined as the single point (the single 'principle of authority') from which the authority of the pope and the authority of the emperor emerge as two clearly defined and separate entities.

[27] The 'first sin' is the sin of the Fall; that is, disobedience, defined by Adam himself in *Paradiso* XXVI as a 'trapassar del segno' (*Par.*, XXVI. 117), a refusal to accept the limitations imposed by God. The image of the serpent, used here to illustrate the self-destructive nature of such disobedience, is, in this context, particularly appropriate. The image recalls the punishment of Dante's thieves in *Inferno* XXV, and is taken up in letter VII. 7 where Florence is described as 'the viper who turns against the vitals of her own mother'.

[28] Dante's original addresses itself here to two distinct groups. While not clearly distinguished in the body of the letter, the two groups would seem to consist of those who have hitherto rejected Henry's authority (addressed in § 4), and those who, like Dante, have 'suffered injustice' because of their support for him (addressed in § 5).

inhabitants of Italy, who are destined to be not only subjects of his Empire, but also free men under his leadership.

[7] I implore you not just to rise up to meet him, but to come into his presence with awe and wonder. You drink from his rivers and sail on his seas; you walk on the sand of the shores and the peaks of the mountains, and all these things belong to him; it is thanks to the bond of his laws, and for no other reason, that you can enjoy public rights and to possess private goods. Do not delude yourselves like ignorant people, who say in their hearts, as if in a dream: 'We have no Lord.'[29] For everything under the sky is his garden and his lake, since 'the sea belongs to God and he made it, so does the land, he shaped this too'.[30] And it is clear from the miracles that have been performed[31] that God preordained the rule of the Roman emperor, and the Church acknowledges that he later confirmed this through the words of the Word.[32]

[8] Indeed, if 'ever since God created the world his everlasting power and deity – however invisible – have been there for the mind to see in the things he has made',[33] and if that which is unknown is revealed to us through that which is better known,[34] if, put quite simply, human understanding is such that, through the movement of the heavens, we can comprehend their Mover and His will, then

---

[29] Compare Psalm 13. 1 [14. 1]: 'The fool says in his heart, "There is no God!" '. The numbering of the Psalms in this edition is that of the Vulgate. The numbering of the Authorized Version is given in square brackets.

[30] Psalm 94. 5 [95. 5]. This same passage is quoted in *Monarchia*, III. xv. 6, in explanation of Christ's statement that 'my kingdom is not of this world' (John 18. 36), which – Dante explains – 'is not to be understood to mean that Christ, who is God, is not Lord of this kingdom, for the Psalmist says "The sea is his, and he made it: and his hands formed the dry land"; but that, as the model for the church, he had no concern for this kingdom.'

[31] This sentence anticipates the conclusion of the discussion, which will be elaborated in the letter's final two paragraphs. The miracles which reveal God's hand in Roman history will be discussed in more detail in §§ 8-9, below.

[32] Christ's confirmation of Roman authority will be discussed in more detail in §§ 9-10, below. For Christ as 'the Word', see John 1. 1-14.

[33] Romans 1. 20. Dante quotes this same passage in *Monarchia*, II. ii. 8.

[34] See *Convivio*, II. i. 13: 'Onde, si come dice lo Filosofo nel primo della Fisica, la natura vuole che ordinatamente si proceda ne la nostra conoscenza, cioè procedendo da quello che conoscemo meglio in quello che conoscemo non così bene.'

this predestination will be perfectly clear even to the most casual observer. For if we go back over the events of the past from the first spark which ignited this fire (namely, from the time when hospitality was denied to the Argives by the Phrygians),[35] taking the opportunity to look again at the history of the world until the triumphs of Octavian,[36] we will see that some of these events have clearly gone beyond the highest achievements of human virtue,[37] and that God has worked through human beings, as if through new heavens.[38] For we do not always act of our own accord, but rather we are sometimes God's instruments; and the human will, which is, by its very nature, free,[39] can nonetheless sometimes be made immune to baser influences and subject only to the eternal will of God, which it serves, often without realizing it.

[9] And if these fundamental arguments are not enough to confirm what we are trying to prove, surely nobody could disagree with me as to the conclusion to be drawn from these premises, that is to say, the fact that after a twelve-year peace which embraced the

---

[35] The Argives are the Argonauts or Greeks; the Phrygians are the Trojans. The reference is to the Trojan King, Laomedon, turning away the Argonauts at the port of Simois, an action which was – in the long term – to lead to the Trojan war (and thus ultimately to the founding of Rome by Aeneas). See, for example, Brunetto Latini's account of this event in *Tresor*, I. 32: 'Dou roi Ilus nasqui Laomedon, qui vea les porz à Jason [...] et à ses autres compaignons qui aloient por la thoison d'or. Dont il avint puis que Jason et Hercules, o tout l'ost des Grezois vindrent à Troie et destruistrent la terre.'

[36] That is to say, Augustus, who, for Dante, personifies the Empire at its greatest point, as will be seen in § 9 below.

[37] See *Monarchia*, II. iv. 5: 'That God performed miracles so that the Roman empire might be supreme is confirmed by the testimony of illustrious authors.' Dante goes on to mention (among other examples) the geese who saved the Capitol from being taken by the Gauls, the sudden hailstorm which saved the city from invasion by Hannibal and the swimming of the Tiber by Cloelia.

[38] The idea of the 'new heaven' may perhaps be drawn from Isaiah 65. 17 ('For now I create new heavens and a new earth'), but it also recalls Virgil's prophecy of the return to a Golden Age, frequently interpreted in the Middle Ages (as it is, most famously, by Dante's Statius) as a prophecy of the coming of Christ (see *Eclogue* IV. 6 and *Purg.*, XXII. 70-72).

[39] See *Monarchia*, I. xii, where Dante argues that human beings are best able to exercise this faculty of free will – and therefore are most happy – under the government of a Monarch. See also *Paradiso*, V. 19-22: 'Lo maggior don che Dio per sua larghezza | fesse creando [...] | fu della volontà la libertate.'

whole world, the face of the Son of God, the world's syllogizer,[40] was revealed, appearing as the culminating point of this process.[41] And when this Son of God was made man for the revelation of the Spirit and was preaching the gospel on earth, he appeared to divide the whole world into two kingdoms, his own and that of Caesar, and ordained that to each should be given the things that belonged to him.[42]

[10] Furthermore, if some intransigent soul who is not yet willing to accept the truth should demand more, let him consider the words of Christ, when he was already under arrest, for when Pilate asserted his authority over him, our Light declared that the power which Pilate – acting as the Emperor's representative in that place – claimed to hold actually came from above.[43] Therefore, do not 'go on living the aimless kind of life that Pagans live',

---

[40] This unusual way of referring to Christ draws on the syllogism, a form of argument characteristic of Aristotelian logic, which allows a valid inference to be deduced from two premises. A syllogism consists of three statements: a major premise, a minor premise and a conclusion. Once the major and minor premises have been shown to be true, the conclusion must necessarily follow as a natural consequence. Here then, Christ is presented as the natural, logical consequence of the fact that God had worked through human beings, via a series of miraculous occurrences, to establish world peace in the time of Augustus. Interestingly, Dante here seems to conflate reason (the syllogistic explanation for Christ's coming) with revelation (Christ was 'made man for the revelation of the Spirit'), bringing together – as he does so frequently in these letters – imperial with providential history.

[41] This argument is also put forward in *Monarchia*, I. xvi. 1, where Dante discusses the 'remarkable historical fact' of the 'state of humanity which the Son of God either awaited, or himself chose to bring about, when he was on the point of becoming man for the salvation of mankind. For if we review the ages and dispositions of men from the fall of our first parents [...], we shall not find that there ever was peace throughout the world except under the immortal Augustus, when a perfect monarchy existed.' A possible source for this view is found in Orosius: 'So at that time, that is, in that year in which, by the ordination of God, Caesar achieved the strongest and truest peace, Christ was born, upon whose coming that peace waited' (*Seven Books of History Against the Pagans*, VI. 22).

[42] This is a clear reference to Christ's answer to the Pharisees, who had asked him whether it was permissible to pay taxes to Caesar: 'Give back to Caesar what belongs to Caesar – and to God what belongs to God' (Matthew 22. 21).

[43] 'Pilate then said to him: "Are you refusing to speak to me? Surely you know I have power to release you and I have power to crucify you?". "You would have no power over me" replied Jesus "if it had not been given you from above [...]"' (John 19. 10-11).

obscured by shadows,[44] but open your minds' eyes and see that the Lord of heaven and earth has appointed a king for us. This is he whom Peter, the Vicar of Christ, orders us to honour,[45] and whom Clement, Peter's current successor, has graced with his apostolic benediction,[46] so that the radiance of the lesser light may bring illumination wherever the spiritual light proves insufficient.[47]

---

[44] Ephesians 5. 17-18: 'In particular, I want to urge you in the name of the Lord, not to go on living the aimless kind of life that pagans live. Intellectually they are in the dark, and they are estranged from the life of God.'

[45] See I Peter 2. 13-17: 'For the sake of the Lord, accept the authority of every social institution: the emperor, as the supreme authority, and the governors as commissioned by him to punish criminals and praise good citizenship. [...] Have respect for everyone and love for our community; fear God and honour the emperor.'

[46] Pope Clement V had issued an encyclical (*Divinae Sapientiae*) in July 1309, approving the election of Henry VII. On 1 September 1310, a second encyclical (*Exultet in Gloria*) was issued, in which Clement called upon Christians – and Italians in particular – to receive and honour Henry.

[47] See *Monarchia*, III. iv, in which Dante refutes the opinion of those who argue that the Empire is subordinate to the Papacy as the moon is subordinate to the sun: 'Firstly they say, basing themselves on *Genesis*, that God created "two great lights" – a greater light and a lesser light – so that one might rule the day and the other rule the night; these they took ion an allegorical sense to mean the two powers, i.e. the spiritual and the temporal. They then go on to argue that, just as the moon, which is the lesser light, has no light except that which it receives from the sun, in the same way the temporal power has now authority except that which it receives from the spiritual power' (III. iv. 2-3). In the rest of this chapter – as, indeed, in the whole of book III – Dante systematically refutes this notion and puts forward his own idea of the Papacy and the Empire as equal, but separate, authorities ('due soli' as in *Purgatorio*, XVI. 106-08).

The Letter to the Florentines (Letter VI)

Introduction: 31 March 1311

The date of this letter is given in the text itself. It was written on 31 March 1311, when it is thought that Dante was staying with Count Guido Novello di Battifolle at the castle of Poppi in the Casentino to the east of Florence.

In the period between December 1310 and March 1311 Henry VII had started to become aware of some of the difficulties that were to render his Italian campaign more complex than he had originally expected. He had been crowned in Milan on 6 January 1311 amid optimistic celebrations. Florence, however, had refused to send representatives to the coronation, and instead made large gifts to members of the Papal court and to Robert of Anjou in a blatant attempt to garner support for a possible future conflict with Henry. In particular, Florence objected to the way in which Henry had restored Ghibelline exiles to Guelph-dominated cities in Lombardy and had replaced local leaders with his own imperial vicars.[1]

And it was not only Florence, it seems, which found these measures unacceptable. By mid-February 1311 discontent was spreading through the Lombard cities, and in Crema, Brescia, Cremona, Reggio, Parma, and Lodi the Ghibellines whom Henry had allowed to return were once again violently expelled. Crema, Brescia, Cremona, and Reggio also expelled their imperial vicars, to all intents and purposes restoring Guelph rule. Henry was able to put down these rebellions and to restore peace and order, but the resistance expressed here set a new tone, very different from the enthusiastic acclamation which had greeted Henry in the last months of 1310.[2]

Meanwhile, Florence continued to look for ways to preserve its own independence. A letter sent to Henry by Clement V on 30 March 1311 (just a day before the date of Dante's letter to the Florentines) confirms that Florentine ambassadors had been lobbying the Pope at Avignon to support them in these claims to independence since before Christmas 1310. In his letter, Clement

---

[1] See Bowsky, *Henry VII in Italy*, pp. 78-82.

[2] See Bowsky, *Henry VII in Italy*, pp. 96-105.

urges Henry to accede to the Florentines' requests. At the same time, the Florentine commune stopped referring to Henry in its official documents as 'King of the Romans' or 'Emperor-elect' and instead gave him the title of 'King of the Germans' in a fairly clumsy attempt to keep Henry's authority at a safe distance.[3] On 1 April 1311 (the day after the date of Dante's letter) Florence sent new instructions to its ambassadors in Avignon, stating that Florence would no longer even allow Henry to enter its territories.

It is this resistance to Henry that forms the background to this letter. Dante criticizes Florence for its attempts to claim the prescriptive right to rule its lands independently of the Empire. He laments the presumption which allows Florence to set herself up as an equal authority to the Empire and the absurdity of wanting to see 'two moons in the sky' (VI. 2), two equal secular authorities competing for jurisdiction over the same territory. He points out the dire consequences for Italy in general and for Florence in particular of resisting Henry's divinely willed mission, prophesying the total destruction of the city if it persists in its rebellious position, and he urges Florence to accept Henry as her Lord, in order that her citizens 'should enjoy the peace that only the stability of such a government can guarantee' (VI. 1).

---

[3] See Bowsky, *Henry VII in Italy*, pp. 110-11.

Letter VI

Letter VI

From Dante Alighieri, a Florentine undeservedly in exile, to the most wicked Florentines within the city.[1]

[1] The faithful providence of the Eternal King, whose goodness sustains the heavenly things above, yet who does not forsake in disdain the things of this world here below, has ordained that human affairs should be governed by the Holy Roman Empire, in order that human beings should enjoy the peace that only the stability of such a government can guarantee, and should live in citizenship with one another throughout the world, in accordance with the will of nature.[2] Although this much is attested by the divine word,[3] and borne out by the writers of antiquity, relying on the evidence of reason alone,[4] nonetheless, the truth of the matter is

---

[1] Dante the exile here addresses his direct political opponents, the Black Guelphs who had exiled him and who aimed to ally Florence ever more closely with the Papacy. Note that despite the opposition between Dante, the outsider, and those Florentines who remain 'within the city', Dante continues to refer to himself as 'a Florentine' (compare *Convivio*, II. vi. 8: 'chiamare solemo la cittade quelli che la tengono, e non coloro che la combattono, avvegna che l'uno e l'altro sia cittadino').

[2] The argument that the Empire is necessary in order to guarantee peace and therefore happiness ('la vita felice') to all its citizens is reiterated by Dante in both the *Convivio* and the *Monarchia*. 'Il perché, a queste guerre e a le loro cagioni torre via, conviene di necessitade tutta la terra, e quanto a l'umana generazione a possedere è dato, essere Monarchia cioè uno solo prencipato, e uno prencipe avere; lo quale, tutto possedendo e più desiderare non possendo, li regi tegna contenti ne li termini de li regni, sì che pace intra loro sia, ne la quale si posino le cittadi, e in questa posa le vicinanze s'amino, in questo amore le case prendano ogni loro bisogno, lo qual preso, l'uomo viva felicemente; che è quello per che esso è nato' (*Conv.*, IV. iv. 4); 'it is agreed that the whole of mankind is ordered to one goal, as has already been demonstrated: there must therefore be one person who directs and rules mankind, and he is properly called "Monarch" or "Emperor". And thus it is apparent that the well-being of the world requires that there be a monarchy or empire' (*Mon.*, I. v. 9-10).

[3] That is, by the writings of the Bible. See *Monarchia*, III. iv. 11: 'For although there are many who record the divine word, it is God alone who dictates, deigning to reveal his pleasure to us through the pens of many men.'

[4] 'That God performed miracles so that the Roman empire might be supreme is confirmed by the testimony of illustrious authors' (*Mon.*, II. iv. 5). The examples which follow in this chapter of the *Monarchia* are taken from Livy, Lucan, and Virgil.

confirmed once and for all by the fact that when the throne of Augustus is vacant, the whole world goes awry, the captain and the oarsmen of the ship of St Peter fall asleep,[5] and wretched Italy, left alone, at the mercy of private decisions and devoid of any public control, is so battered and buffeted by gales and floods that words cannot describe it, and the abject Italians themselves can scarcely measure it with their tears.[6] Therefore, even if the sword of the one who says 'vengeance is mine'[7] has not yet struck from heaven, let all those who, in their blind arrogance, resist such a clear sign of God's will, now turn pale at the thought of the impending judgment of such a severe judge.

[2] As for you, the awful voracity of your cupidity has ensnared you, so that you are prepared to commit any act of wickedness, in disobedience of both human and divine laws. Are you not tormented by fear of the second death,[8] since you, the first and only ones to dread the burden of liberty, have risen up against the glory of the Roman Prince, the king of the world and God's minister,[9]

---

[5] By 'the ship of St Peter' Dante implies the Church. Compare *Paradiso*, XI. 118-20: 'Pensa oramai qual fu colui che degno | collega fu a mantener la barca | di Pietro', and *Purgatorio*, XXXII. 129, where a voice from Heaven cries out in response to the transformations of the chariot which represents the Church: 'O navicella mia, com' mal se' carca!'.

[6] This sentence contains many parallels with the famous invective against Italy in *Purgatorio* VI. In the invective, Italy is 'serva' (line 76) and 'misera' (line 85), just as here Italy is 'wretched' and the Italians 'abject'. The image of the ship unguided by its captain and oarsmen is echoed by Dante's description of Italy as a 'nave sanza nocchiere in gran tempesta' (line 77), and this line also recalls the buffeting of gales and floods referred to here. Likewise, the mention of the vacant throne of Augustus, recalls Dante's attack, in the invective, on the abandonment of Rome by 'Alberto tedesco' (line 97) and the reference to the 'sella [...] vota' (line 89) of the Empire. And just as Italy here is described as being 'alone', so too in the invective it is Rome which is 'vedova e sola' in the absence of her 'Cesare' (lines 113-14).

[7] That is, God; see Deuteronomy 32. 35.

[8] That is, the death of the soul or eternal damnation, as Virgil explains to Dante's pilgrim at the start of his otherworldly journey: 'vedrai li antichi spiriti dolenti, | ch'a la seconda morte ciascun grida' (*Inf.*, I. 116-17). Compare Revelation 21. 8: 'But the legacy for cowards, for those who break their word, or worship obscenities, for murderers and fornicators, and for fortune-tellers, idolaters or any other sort of liars, is the second death in the burning lake of sulphur'.

[9] Compare Psalm 2. 1-2: 'Why this uproar among the nations? Why this impotent muttering of pagans – kings on earth rising in revolt, princes plotting against

and, claiming prescriptive rights and denying your obligation to show him due subservience,[10] have preferred to rebel against him in mad revolt? Are you unaware, in your absurd perversity,[11] that public rights cannot be restricted by arguments based on prescription and can only be brought to an end with the end of time itself? Public authority in the political arena can never pass into oblivion, no matter how long it has been neglected. nor can it be called into question no matter how weakened it may be, as is unquestionably proved by the holy statutes of the law, and borne out, after due consideration, by human reason. For that which is to the advantage of everybody cannot be destroyed or even simply weakened without being to the detriment of everyone; and this is contrary to the wishes of both God and nature, and all human beings would concur in finding it deeply abhorrent. Now that you have been made aware of the foolishness of such an opinion, why do you insist on forsaking the holy Empire and on trying to build new kingdoms, like second Babylonians,[12] as if the politics of

---

Yahweh and his Anointed.' These verses are also quoted by Dante in full at the opening of book II of the *Monarchia*, and obviously serve to underline the divinely willed role of the Roman Empire (and, in this case, specifically of Henry VII) for Dante.

[10] Prescriptive rights are those claimed over a territory by a new ruler, after an extended period of rule with no challenge from the original sovereign. By claiming such rights, the new ruler or government assumes that the 'rightful' sovereign's negligence of the territory represents a *de facto* agreement to the transfer of sovereignty to the new ruler. In the face of, first, Henry's ambassadors (who visited the city in July 1310) and then of Henry himself, Florence insisted that, while it was willing to acknowledge Henry as the rightful Emperor, it was not willing to give up its long-held independence, nor its control of the surrounding dependent territories in its *contado*. Thus Florence is claiming a prescriptive right to self-government, as opposed to the 'public rights' which the Emperor holds over all imperial territories.

[11] The Latin term used here is the rare *discoli*: 'amentes et discoli' (literally: absurd and unfair). The word is found in the Vulgate in I Peter 2. 18: 'Slaves must be respectful and obedient to their masters, not only when they are kind and gentle, but also when they are unfair' ['non tantum bonis et modestis sed etiam discolis']. Dante's use of this term, which is not used in Classical Latin, reinforces the strongly biblical tone of the letter.

[12] That is, like the builders of Babel (traditionally conflated with Babylon in the Middle Ages). Compare St Augustine, *City of God*, XVI. 4: 'This city which was called "Confusion" is none other than Babylon [...]. The name "Babylon" means, in fact, "confusion". [...] But what could the empty presumption of man have

Florence were one thing and that of Rome something quite different? Why do you not regard the Church with similar envy? If you would like to see two moons in the sky, why not also two suns?[13] And so, even if the crimes which you have dared to commit do not fill you with fear, then the fact that, as a punishment for your sins you have been deprived not only of wisdom but also of the very beginning of wisdom,[14] should strike terror into your obdurate hearts. Indeed, the most dreadful behaviour that a sinner can exhibit is that of doing whatever he pleases, without shame or fear of God. And this is, undoubtedly, a punishment often inflicted on the wicked, so that those who in life have closed their eyes to God, in dying close their eyes on themselves.

[3] Has your presumptuous arrogance deprived you, like the mountains of Gilboa,[15] of that dew which falls from heaven, to such an extent that not only do you remain unworried at having resisted the decree of the eternal Senate, but neither, moreover, are you worried by your own lack of fear? If so, do you also expect to remain untouched by that fear of destruction which is human and this-worldly, now that the inevitable sorry end of your proud blood and of the pillage which has caused so much grief is fast approaching? Or do you believe that you can somehow defend yourselves from behind your pathetic fortifications?[16] Oh you, who

---

achieved, no matter how vast the structure it contrived, whatever the height to which that building towered into the sky in its challenge to God?'.

[13] There is a classical reference here, in the original Latin, which asks: 'if you would like to see Delia duplicated in the sky, why not also Delius?'. Delia and Delius are alternative names for Diana (the goddess of the moon) and Apollo (the god of the sun). The reference to the moon and the sun takes up that at the end of letter V (see note 47 to letter V in this edition) and in book III of the *Monarchia*.

[14] See Psalm 111. 10: 'This fear of Yahweh is the beginning of wisdom'.

[15] See II Samuel 1. 21: 'O mountains of Gilboa, let there be no dew or rain on you; treacherous fields, for there the hero's shield was dishonoured.'

[16] Villani reports that in November 1310 the Florentines ordered that their city should be fortified n order to protect it against a potential assault by Henry VII: 'i Fiorentini per tema della venuta dello 'mperadore sì ordinarono a chiudere la città di fossi da la porta a San Gallo infino a la porta di Santo Ambruogio [...] e poi infino al fiume d'Arno: e poi, da la porta di San Gallo infino a quella dal Prato d'Ognesanti erano già fondate le mura, sì le feciono inalzare VIII braccia. E questo lavoro fu fatto sùbito e in poco tempo, la qual cosa fermamente fu poi lo scampo de la città di Firenze [...]; imperciò che la città era tutta schiusa, e le mura vecchie

are united only in doing evil! Oh you, who have been blinded by your extraordinary cupidity![17] When that terrible eagle in its field of gold[18] – the eagle which soars now over the Pyrenees, now over the Caucasus, now over the Atlas mountains,[19] borne up and sustained by the heavenly host, and which, in ancient times, gazed down from his flight upon the vast expanses of the oceans – comes swooping down upon you, what good will it do you to have hidden behind your defences, or to have ordered the city to be fortified with bulwarks and battlements? What good will it do you, you most despicable of people, when you stand, overwhelmed, in the presence of the one who is coming to subdue Italy's reckless folly?[20] Your rebellion will certainly do nothing to advance the unwarranted hopes which you nurture in vain. Rather, your opposition will only further provoke the just king when he comes, so that the mercy which always accompanies his army will fly away in indignation; and while you believe yourselves to be defending the threshold of false liberty,[21] instead you will be thrown into the prison of true slavery. For indeed we believe that sometimes, through God's miraculous judgement, it happens that the means whereby the wicked person attempts to avoid the

---

quasi gran parte disfatte, e vendute a' prossimani vicini per allargare la città vecchia, e chiudere i borghi e la giunta nuova' (*Nuova cronica*, X. 10).

[17] Dante's attack on the Florentines here ('O male concordes! o mira cupidine obcecati!') echoes very precisely that of Lucan on the Roman triumvirate whom he blames for the outbreak of the civil war: 'O male concordes, nimiaque cupidine caeci' [Oh you who are united in doing evil and blinded by too much cupidity] (*Pharsalia*, I. 87; my translation).

[18] The imperial standard was a black eagle on a gold background. See *Purgatorio*, X. 80-81: 'e l'aguglie ne l'oro | sovr'essi in vista al vento si movieno'.

[19] The three mountain ranges indicate the boundaries of the Empire (at least ideally) to the West, East, and South respectively.

[20] Italy here is referred to as 'Hesperia', a Greek term, meaning generically 'west', but used in the ancient world to refer to Italy (and/or sometimes also to the Iberian peninsula).

[21] The Latin term, translated here as 'threshold', is *trabea*, which carried the meaning, in the Classical period, of a 'robe of state', a special toga worn by rulers, consuls and augurs. In translations of this passage, the word is sometimes translated with this meaning. Toynbee, however, suggests that the word is used here in the medieval sense of a 'porch', a meaning which seems, perhaps, more apt in this context. Uguccione da Pisa confirms this meaning: '**trabea** autem dicitur porticus tuta' [**trabea** is also held to mean a porch] (*Derivationes*, II. 132).

punishment which he deserves becomes the very means by which he is more directly driven towards it, and that the person who intentionally and willingly resists God's will may in fact, unintentionally and unwillingly, be serving it.

[4] To your anguish, you will see the buildings, which you did not erect prudently according to your needs, but rather developed recklessly for your own pleasure,[22] destroyed by battering-rams and burned by fire, since no second Troy encircles them with its walls. Now the population, divided against itself, rages indiscriminately, some for you and some against you, but then you will see it united in raising its voice terribly in opposition to you, since a starving mob is incapable of fear.[23] Likewise you will be ashamed to see your holy places, where groups of women congregate each day, defiled, and your children, bewildered and ignorant, destined to pay for the sins of their fathers.[24] And if my prophetic gift does not deceive me[25] in foretelling what it has been shown both by unequivocal signs and by unquestionable arguments, then once the majority of your citizens has been lost, either through death or through captivity, those few who are left to endure exile will see, through their tears, the city, worn out by its protracted mourning, finally handed over to strangers. In short, the misfortunes which the glorious city of Saguntum endured, in its

---

[22] This passage is reminiscent of Cacciaguida's criticism, in *Paradiso* XV, of the Florence of Dante's day, which – in contrast to the modest city of his own time – aims to outdo Rome in the grandeur and size of its buildings (far exceeding the needs of the citizens who inhabited them): 'Non avea case di famiglia vòte; | non v'era giunto ancor Sardanapalo | a mostrar ciò che 'n camera si puote. | Non era vinto ancora Montemalo | dal vostro Uccellatoio, che, com'è vinto | nel montar sú, cosí sarà nel calo.' (*Par.*, XV. 106-11).

[23] See Lucan, *Pharsalia*, III. 58: 'a starving people is incapable of fear'.

[24] 'I punish the father's fault in the sons, the grandsons and the great-grandsons of those who hate me' (Exodus 20. 5). 'Our fathers have sinned; they are no more, and we ourselves bear the weight of their crimes' (Lamentations 5. 7). See also *Paradiso*, VI. 109-10: 'Molte fïate già pianser li figli | per la colpa del padre'. In this final passage too the context is that of a criticism of Florence, coming at the climax of Justinian's invective against the Guelphs and Ghibellines.

[25] Compare Forese Donati's 'l'antiveder qui non m'inganna' (*Purg.*, XXIII. 109), and note Dante's self-presentation as a prophet in this passage.

LETTER VI

loyalty, for the sake of liberty, you too, in your *dis*loyalty, will suffer, but ignominiously, not for freedom, but to become slaves.[26]

[5] And do not take heart from the unexpected success of the people of Parma, who, at the seductive urging of hunger, whispered to one another, 'let us rather rush down into the middle of the battle and die', and made an attack on Caesar's encampment, while Caesar was away.[27] For although they were victorious at Vittoria, they nonetheless memorably reaped pain as a reward for the pain they sowed there.[28] But consider the thunderbolts of Frederick I, and take counsel from Milan and from Spoleto,[29] because, at the

---

[26] Saguntum, near the city of Valencia, was besieged by Hannibal in 219 BC in an incident which sparked the Second Punic War. St Augustine's account of the city's loyalty to Rome is particularly suggestive: 'This Spanish city, a firm friend of the Roman people, was overthrown for keeping faith with Rome. For when Hannibal broke his treaty with Rome and was seeking occasion to provoke Rome to war, he began by laying fierce siege to Saguntum. [...] At first the community was wasted by famine, it is even said that many of them ate the dead bodies of their dear ones. Then, when they were completely exhausted, the Saguntines, intending at all costs to avoid falling captive into the hands of Hannibal, erected a huge pyre in a public place, set it on fire and, in mutual slaughter, committed themselves and their fellows to the flames' (*City of God*, III. 20). The heroic self-sacrifice of the Saguntines in the service of Rome thus shows up particularly clearly the arrogant and selfish self-destructiveness of the contemporary Florentines.

[27] This is a reference to the victory of the people of Parma over the Emperor Frederick II in 1248. Frederick had set up an encampment (nicknamed 'Vittoria') outside Parma, and was laying siege to the city. Starving and desperate, the people got wind of the fact that Frederick was absent on a hunting expedition and attacked his camp, taking the *carroccio* of Cremona (which supported the Emperor) and Frederick's crown and imperial standard, with the ensuing disgrace which such a loss incurred on the imperial side. (See Salimbene's *Chronicle*, pp. 193-94.)

[28] Parma's forces were later defeated by the Imperial side and the city's *carroccio* lost to Cremona. 'Yet because of their sins and the adverse times, the Parmese within the city still suffered a great misfortune: the enemy captured their carroccio, which they had deserted in the street, and three thousand of their infantry and many knights were killed' (Salimbene, *Chronicle*, p. 335).

[29] The city of Milan was destroyed by Frederick I in 1162, as Dante mentions in *Purgatorio*, XVIII. 119-20: 'sotto lo 'mperio del buon Barbarossa, | di cui dolente ancor Milan ragiona'. The city of Spoleto was destroyed in 1155, in the first year of Frederick's reign (see Villani, *Nuova cronica*, V. 1). In the notes to the Ricciardi edition, Frugoni points out the suggestive inversion of chronological order in this sequence (from 1248 to 1162 to 1155) through which Dante encourages the reader to cast his/her mind backwards in time.

thought of their disobedience and equally of their unmitigated destruction, your puffed-up flesh will grow cold, and your impetuous hearts will shrink back in fear. Oh most deluded of Tuscans, irrational by nature and made even more irrational by corruption! In your ignorance, you neither contemplate nor envisage how, in the eyes of those who are fully-fledged,[30] *the net is cast in vain*,[31] as the feet of your unsound minds go astray in the shadows of the night.[32] Indeed, you appear to those who are fully-fledged and to those of blameless life[33] as if you were standing on the threshold of a prison, driving away anyone who shows you pity, lest perhaps he might set you free from the captivity in which you are shackled with chains and fetters.[34] Nor do you notice, in your blindness, the hold that your cupidity has over you, cajoling you with poisonous whispers and restraining you with deceitful threats. Indeed, it has made you prisoners of the law of sin,[35] and has forbidden you to obey those most sacred laws which are made

---

[30] 'Those who are fully-fledged' is clearly a reference to the adult bird as opposed to the chick, and thus to people who have attained a certain degree of maturity. Compare *Purgatorio*, XXXI. 61-63: 'Novo augelletto due o tre aspetta; | ma dinanzi da li occhi d'i pennuti | rete si spiega indarno o si saetta.'

[31] The words in italics are absent from the manuscript of this letter (Vaticano Pal. Lat. 1729). Their addition was suggested by Pistelli (*Bullettino della Società Dantesca Italiana*, 24 (1917), p. 64), though others have contested the validity and necessity of this addition (and, indeed, the sentence makes sense without the added words). Pistelli's thesis is supported by the echoes of his suggested interpolation in the lines from *Purgatorio* XXXI quoted above, and in the passage from Proverbs quoted below.

[32] This sentence is very reminiscent of the warning issued in Proverbs 1. 15-18: 'My son, do not follow them in their way, keep your steps out of their path (for their feet hasten to evil, they are quick to shed blood); the net is always spread in vain if the bird is watching. It is for their own blood these men lie in wait, their own selves they lie in ambush for.' Again, the theme of self-destructiveness here is very much in keeping with the warning which Dante issues to the Florentines in this letter.

[33] The Latin here, 'inmaculati in via', is a quotation from the opening verse of Psalm 118 [119]: 'Ah, how happy those of blameless life who walk in the Law of Yahweh!'.

[34] Compare Psalm 149. 8: '[...] to shackle their kings with chains and their nobles with fetters'.

[35] See Romans 7. 23: 'This is what makes me a prisoner of that law of sin which lives inside my body.'

in the image of natural justice, laws whose observance – if it is joyful and free – not only can be seen to involve no element of coercion, but rather, on closer inspection, reveals itself to be nothing less than perfect liberty itself. For what is this liberty if not the free translation of the will into action, which the laws facilitate for those who obey them? Therefore, since only those who obey the laws of their own free will are truly free, who do you think you are, who pretend to love liberty, but who break all laws in conspiring against the Prince who is source of the law?

[6] You most worthless offspring of Fiesole![36] You savages, now punished once again![37] Is this presage perhaps not frightening enough for you? I fully believe that, although you simulate hope on your faces and in your lying words, you lie awake at night, trembling, and when you do sleep you often wake terrified by the presentiments conveyed to you in your dreams or with your mind going back over the day's decisions. But if, in your justified terror, you repent of your madness, yet without remorse, then, in order that the little streams of fear and remorse flow together into the bitter river of penitence, it should be enough for you to bear in mind that he who sustains the Roman commonwealth,[38] the holy

---

[36] Compare *Inferno*, XV. 61-62: 'Ma quello ingrato popolo maligno | che discese di Fiesole *ab* antico.' In Dante's time, the most pervasive legend relating to the foundation of Florence told how the city had been founded by Julius Caesar at the time of Catiline's rebellion against the Roman Republic. The Roman general, Florinus, was killed while besieging Catiline in Fiesole. His death was avenged by the Roman forces, who sacked the Etruscan city and resettled its inhabitants in the Arno valley, in a new city named Florentia in memory of the dead general. The 'sementa santa' (*Inf.*, XV. 76) of the Romans, which lives on in Dante, is thus opposed to the anti-Roman feelings embodied by the descendents of the rebellious Fiesolans, in a struggle whose repercussions stretch across the centuries.

[37] Fiesole had been rebuilt, in symbolic defiance of Rome, by the barbarian Totila (often confused with Attila, as is the case in *Inferno* XIII), who also destroyed Florence and many other Roman towns. The Roman rebuilding of Florence after this setback is alluded to by Dante's anonymous Florentine suicide, who speaks of 'que' cittadin che poi la rifondarno | sovra 'l cener che d'Attila rimase' (*Inf.*, XIII. 148-49).

[38] The term used in Latin here is *baiulus*, which echoes that used by Dante for the rulers of Rome in both the *Convivio* and the *Commedia*. Compare *Convivio*, IV. v. 11: 'li sette regi che prima la [Rome] governaro [...] che furono quasi baiuli e tutori de la sua puerizia', and *Paradiso*, VI. 73: 'quel che fé col baiulo seguente'. In the latter case, the reference is to Augustus, the supreme example of Roman imperial strength for Dante, and the most perfect model for the imperial revival which Dante hoped to see brought about by Henry VII.

and triumphant Henry, not desiring his own advantage, but the public good, has, for our sakes, willingly accepted his difficult task, sharing in our pain, as if the prophet Isaiah had been pointing the finger of prophecy at him, after Christ, when, through the revelation of the holy spirit he prophesied that 'ours were the sufferings he bore, ours the sorrows he carried'.[39] You must, therefore, understand – and you are lying if you claim otherwise – that the time for most bitter repentance for your thoughtless presumption is at hand. But a belated repentance of this sort[40] will not buy you forgiveness, but rather will mark the beginning of your timely punishment. So be it; for the sinner will be struck through so that he will surely die before he can make amends.[41]

Written on 31 March,[42] on the border of Tuscany, beneath the source of the Arno,[43] in the first year of the Emperor Henry's most auspicious descent into Italy.[44]

---

[39] Isaiah 53. 4. Once again, Dante underlines the parallels between Henry and Christ. Like Christ, Henry is coming for the good of all human beings, and will suffer pain and rejection in the fulfilment of his God-given task.

[40] That is, without true remorse. See II Corinthians 7. 10: 'To suffer in God's way means changing for the better and leaves no regrets, but to suffer as the world knows suffering brings death'.

[41] The reference here seems to be to I Samuel 14. 38-39: 'Consider carefully where today's sin may lie; for as Yahweh lives who gives victory to Israel, even if it be in Jonathan my son, he shall be put to death'. The Latin of the manuscript has been altered here, following a suggestion by Moore (*Studies in Dante*, IV, 281-83), which is followed in most modern editions of this letter. The original reading 'sine retractatione rivantur' (they are led off) seems nonsensical. Although other suggested readings have been put forward, Moore's suggestion ('sine retractatione moriatur') has the weight of biblical authority, because of the clear echo of the passage given above.

[42] Literally, the day before the Calends (that is, the first day) of April.

[43] It is thought that Dante was staying, at the time he wrote this letter, with Count Guido Novello di Battifolle at the castle of Poppi in the Casentino to the east of Florence. The source of the Arno is on Mount Falterona in the Tuscan Apennines; Poppi is situated some 25 km below the source, on the river itself. The mention of the river here suggests that the exiled Dante imagines his words floating downstream to the ears of the 'wicked Florentines within the city'.

[44] That is, 1311.

The Letter to the Emperor Henry VII (Letter VII)

Introduction: 17 April 1311

Like letter VI, this letter contains precise information about its date and place of composition. It was written on 17 April 1311, only just over two weeks after the letter to the Florentines, while Dante was still at Poppi. The tone of frustration and anger with Florence which characterise the previous letter also emerges here, but in this case the letter is addressed to Henry VII himself, whom Dante urges to move against the rebellious Florentines before it is too late.

After his coronation in Milan – which may have been the occasion recalled by Dante in this letter, when he personally paid homage to the Emperor (VII. 2) – Henry had spent some time drawing up peace settlements for the cities of Lombardy and ensuring that these were put into effect. He had also, in anticipation of his journey south, appointed his brother-in-law Count Amadeus V of Savoy to the post of Vicar-General in Lombardy, with responsibility for the administration of the whole of northern Italy, from Piedmont to the Veneto, in Henry's absence. These preparations assumed that Henry would leave Lombardy for Rome in mid-February with a view to being crowned Emperor as soon as possible, bringing forward the date of his Roman coronation, originally set by Clement V for 2 February 1312.[1]

On the day before the imperial party was due to depart for Rome, however, a rebellion broke out in Milan, and uprisings against the Emperor rapidly spread throughout the cities of Lombardy. Departure for Rome was delayed while Henry resolved these difficulties. At the same time, Henry received a response from Clement V rejecting Henry's request that the coronation date be brought forward. By time that Dante wrote his letter, Henry had put down most of the rebellions against him, but the situations in Cremona and Brescia remained to be resolved. Henry entered Cremona on 26 April 1311 and remained there until mid-May, when he set up camp outside the walls of Brescia. The siege of Brescia lasted from 19 May until 19 September, during which time

---

[1] See Bowsky, *Henry VII in Italy*, pp. 94-95.

the Emperor's army was massively reduced in strength and numbers by an outbreak of plague.[2]

In this letter, Dante expresses the view that Henry's problems in Lombardy are of secondary importance compared to the greater threat that he faces in Tuscany. He compares the cities of Lombardy to the heads of the legendary hydra (VII. 6). No sooner will Henry stamp out one rebellion than another two will spring up in its place, delaying him in the north, perhaps indefinitely. Rather, Dante feels that Henry should leave the north in the hands of his Vicar General, and devote his attention to the 'ill-omened beast' on the Arno. Only by conquering Florence, Dante believes, will Henry be able to guarantee a successful coronation in Rome, and a peaceful rule over *all* his territories.

---

[2] For a more detailed account of these events, see Bowsky, *Henry VII in Italy*, pp. 98-125.

Letter VII

To the most holy, most glorious, and most fortunate conqueror and sole lord, the lord Henry, by divine providence king of the Romans and forever Augustus,[1] from his most devoted Dante Alighieri, a Florentine undeservedly in exile, and from all Tuscans who desire peace, who kiss the ground beneath his feet.

[1] As testimony of the infinite love of God, we have been bequeathed peace,[2] in order that the difficulties of our life as members of the Church Militant on earth might be assuaged by its wonderful sweetness, and that, taking advantage of peace on earth, we might earn the bliss of the Church Triumphant in Heaven.[3] But the envy of our ancient and implacable adversary,[4] who always attempts secretly to undermine human happiness, has caused some people to give up of their own free will this inheritance; and, in the absence of our guardian,[5] has ruthlessly stripped it from the rest of us against our will. Hence, for a long time we have wept beside the streams of confusion,[6] and have ceaselessly invoked the protection of our rightful king, praying that he will destroy the brutal tyrant's

---

[1] Dante does not refer to Henry as 'Emperor', but merely as 'king of the Romans', since he has not yet been crowned officially in Rome. His coronation would not take place until 29 June 1312.

[2] 'Peace I bequeath to you, my own peace I give you, a peace the world cannot give, this is my gift to you' (John 14. 27). This passage is quoted explicitly by Dante in *Convivio*, II. xiv. 19.

[3] The references to the Church Militant and the Church Triumphant are implicit, rather than explicit, in Dante's original, which refers to 'militie nostre' (our warfare, our military service) and to 'patrie triumphantis gaudia' (the joy of our triumphant fatherland). It is nonetheless clear that what is implied here is the way in which the ideal political peace for which Dante yearns on earth may be paralleled with the supreme divine peace of Heaven.

[4] That is, the devil, to whom Dante refers in the same terms ('that ancient Adversary') in *Monarchia*, II. ix. 9. Compare also *Purgatorio*, VIII. 95: 'Vedi là 'l nostro avversaro'.

[5] That is, the Emperor, who is referred to literally here as a 'tutor', as in *Convivio*, IV. v. 11, where the early kings of Rome are described as 'quasi baiuli e tutori de la sua puerizia'.

[6] See Psalm 136 [137]. 1: 'Beside the streams of Babylon we sat and wept.' As has been noted, Babylon was, in the Middle Ages, synonymous with 'confusion'. See note 12 to letter VI in this edition.

hangers-on[7] and restore us to justice. So when you, the successor of Caesar and of Augustus, bounded over the Apennines to return the revered Roman standards,[8] immediately our deep sighs stopped and our flood of tears dried up; and, like the rising of a much-desired sun,[9] new hope for a better age for Italy shone out. Then many people, anticipating the fulfilment of their wishes, joined their joyful voices with that of Virgil, and sang of Saturn's reign and the return of the Virgin.[10]

[2] And yet – whether the suggestion be born from the fervour of our desire for him or from some hint of the truth – our sun is now believed to be delaying or suspected of turning back, as if a new Joshua or son of Amoz were giving the orders,[11] so that our

---

[7] Compare § 4 below, where Florence is described at the 'tyrant of Tuscany'. There can, therefore, be little doubt that Florence, her allies and, in particular, the Black Guelphs who control the city (the addressees of letter VI) are intended here.

[8] In the original Latin, the Emperor's standards are referred to, literally, as 'Tarpeian'. This is a reference to the Tarpeian rock on the Capitoline hill in Rome, from which traitors were flung and on which stood the temple to Saturn which contained the Roman Treasury. It is in this context that 'Tarpëa' is referred to by Dante in *Purgatorio*, IX. 137.

[9] In the original Latin, Henry VII is here referred to as 'Titan', as he is in letter V. 1: 'we [...] shall see our long-awaited source of joy, when Titan will rise in peace'.

[10] This is a reference to Virgil's *Eclogue* IV. 6-7, in which he predicts the return to a mythical Golden Age in terms which, to medieval Christian readers, strongly suggested the mystery of the Incarnation: 'Now the Virgin returns, the reign of Saturn returns; now a new generation descends from heaven on high'. The lines are famously translated into Italian by Dante in the tribute of Statius to Virgil in *Purgatorio* XXII: 'Secol si rinova; | torna giustizia e primo tempo umano, | e progenïe scende da ciel nova' (*Purg.*, XXII. 70-72). Here Statius explains that it was precisely reading these lines that led him to be converted to Christianity, explaining his presence in Purgatory rather than (as would have been expected) in Limbo. The fact that Dante almost certainly invented Statius's conversion only increases the relevance of the salvific potential attributed to Virgil's poetry here.

[11] That is, as if time were standing still. The first reference is to Joshua's request for God to stop the progress of the sun until Gibeon had been freed from the control of the Amorites. 'Then Joshua spoke to Yahweh, the same day that Yahweh delivered the Amorites to the Israelites. Joshua declaimed: "Sun stand still over Gibeon, and, moon, you also, over the Vale of Aijalon." And the sun stood still and the moon halted, till the people had vengeance on their enemies. Is this not written in the Book of the Just? The sun stood still in the middle of the sky and delayed its setting for almost a whole day. There was never a day like that before or since, when Yahweh obeyed the voice of a man, for Yahweh was fighting for Israel' (Joshua 10. 12-14). The second reference is to the illness and

uncertainty leads us to doubt, and to burst out with the words of Christ's precursor: 'Are you the one who is to come, or have we got to wait for someone else?'.[12] And, although the frenzy of prolonged desire has a tendency to transform into doubts those things which should be all the more certain for being closer, nonetheless we believe and hope in you, affirming that you are God's minister, the son of the Church, and the guardian of Rome's glories. For I too, who write this letter both in my own name and on behalf of others, saw in you the great benevolence and heard in you the great humility which are fitting to your imperial majesty, when my hands touched your feet, and my lips paid homage to you. Then my spirit exulted in you,[13] and I silently said to myself: 'Behold the lamb of God that takes away the sins of the world'.[14]

[3] Nonetheless, we are astonished by the indolence which so delays you. You were long ago victorious in the Po valley,[15] yet

---

cure of Hezekiah by Isaiah (the 'son of Amoz'). Hezekiah asks for proof that God will cure him of his illness, as he has been promised, and Isaiah causes the shadow to become shorter (thus effectively making time run backwards). See II Kings 20. 1-11.

[12] 'Christ's precursor' is John the Baptist, whose greeting of Christ in these words can be found in Matthew 11. 3 and Luke 7. 19. Just as Christ's reply to John confirms his messianic status, while exhorting his followers to believe in him ('happy is the man who does not lose faith in me'; Matthew 11. 6), so here Dante reiterates the Christological role of Henry VII, and likewise exhorts his followers not to lose faith.

[13] A variant reading of this passage – which is that used by previous English translators – has 'exultavit in *me* spiritus meus', rather than the 'exultavit in te' used for the current version. Both variants echo the words of the *Magnificat* ('my spirit exults in God my saviour'; Luke 1. 47), once again reinforcing the parallels between Henry and Christ. This sentence makes clear that Dante has seen Henry in person and done homage to him, possibly on the occasion of Henry's coronation in Milan on 6 January 1311, although this is not certain.

[14] John 1. 29. Thanks to its role within the liturgy, this passage would have been very well known, and its significance could not have escaped the first readers of the letter. It therefore not only draws yet another parallel between Henry and Christ, but also stands as the climax of a striking accumulation of Christological images in this paragraph.

[15] In another reference to Virgil, the Po valley is described in the Latin original as 'the valley of Eridanus'. In his *Georgics*, Virgil describes the Po as 'Eridanus, king of rivers' (*Georgic* I. 482). In fact, the early part of Henry's campaign in Italy had taken place in Turin, Asti, and Milan, where he had been largely welcomed.

you abandon, forsake, and neglect Tuscany, as if you believed that the imperial authority vested in you extended no further than the borders of Liguria.[16] Indeed, we are led to suspect that you have failed to take into account the fact that the glorious power of the Romans cannot be held in check either within the boundaries of Italy or within the three sides of Europe itself.[17] For although it has been subjected to violence[18] and has drawn back its governance within narrower confines, nonetheless it stretches out everywhere, by uninfringeable right, as far as at the waves of Amphitrite,[19] and the inadequate waters of the ocean can scarcely contain it.[20] In fact, it has been written for our elucidation that there 'shall be born, of proud descent from Troy, one Caesar, to bound his lordship by Ocean's outer stream and his fame by the starry sky'.[21] And when (as we are told by Luke, the evangelist,[22] his words afire with the

---

[16] Liguria seems to be used here in a broad sense to mean northern Italy in general, rather than simply the modern region on the north-west coast.

[17] In the Middle Ages Europe was considered to have a roughly triangular form, whose three points were the Don River (which has a distinctive bend near the town of Volgograd), the pillars of Hercules (that is, the Straits of Gibraltar) and the British Isles: 'Tota autem terra quam nunc describemus, est figurae trigoni circumfusa Oceano mari' [For the whole area which we are now describing is triangular in shape, surrounded by the Ocean] (Albertus Magnus, *De natura loci*, III. 7).

[18] Compare Matthew 11. 12: 'the kingdom of heaven has been subjected to violence'. This sentence therefore reinforces the parallel set up in the first sentence of this letter between Henry's kingdom on earth and the Kingdom of Heaven.

[19] Amphitrite was the queen of the sea in Greek mythology, and the wife of Poseidon. The term is used here metonymically, to refer to the sea itself. Dante uses the term to refer to the 'great ocean' which was thought in medieval cosmology to encircle the inhabited world, and in the *Quaestio de aqua et terra* (XV. 31) he distinguishes this ocean from the sea that lies *within* the boundaries of the inhabited world, the Mediterranean.

[20] Compare *Monarchia*, I. xi. 12: 'But there is nothing the monarch *could* covet, for his jurisdiction is bounded only by the ocean.' The waters of the ocean are 'inadequate' in so far as they would be powerless to prevent the further expansion of the Empire. Also compare letters VI. 3 and XI. 11.

[21] *Aeneid*, I. 286-87. The quotation is a reference to Julius Caesar.

[22] Literally, 'as the lowing of our evangelical bull proclaims'. The bull is traditionally a symbol of St Luke. This image is based on the four beasts referred to in Ezekiel 1. 10 and Revelation 4. 6 ('The first animal was like a lion, the second like a bull, the third animal had a human face, and the fourth animal was

eternal flame) Augustus had decreed that a census should be taken of the whole world,[23] if this decree had not issued from the court of a just ruler, the only son of God[24] – who was made man precisely in order that the nature which he had assumed confirm his subjection to that decree – would not have chosen that moment to be born of the Virgin Mary.[25] For he, for whom it was fitting to do 'all that righteousness demands',[26] would never have advocated an injustice.

[4] Shame on you, therefore – you, to whom the whole world is looking in expectation – for having been caught up for so long in such a small corner of the world; and let it not escape the emperor's watchful gaze that the tyrant of Tuscany[27] is bolstered by its confidence in your continued hesitation, and becomes stronger and stronger day by day by appealing to the pride of the evil-doers, adding insult to injury. Let the words of Curio to Caesar be heard again: 'While your foes are in confusion and before they have gathered strength, make haste; delay is ever fatal to those who are prepared. The toil and danger are no greater than before, but the prize you seek is higher'.[28] And let the words of

---

like a flying eagle'), which were equated with the four evangelists. Dante also refers to these beasts (attaching to them the same interpretation) in *Purgatorio*, XXIX. 92-105.

[23] 'Now at this time Caesar Augustus issued a decree for a census of the whole world to be taken' (Luke 2. 1).

[24] See John 3. 16: 'Yes, God loved the world so much that he gave his only Son, so that everyone who believes in him may not be lost but may have eternal life.'

[25] A fuller version of this same argument is used to prove the legitimacy of Roman authority in *Monarchia*, II. x. 6-7: 'But as his chronicler Luke relates, Christ chose to be born of his Virgin Mother under an edict emanating from Roman authority, so that the Son of God made man might be enrolled as a man in that unique census of the human race; this means that he acknowledged the validity of that edict. And perhaps it is more holy to believe that the edict came by divine inspiration through Caesar, so that he who had been so long awaited in the society of men might himself be enrolled among mortals. Therefore Christ acknowledged by his action that the edict of Augustus, who embodied the authority of the Romans, was legitimate.'

[26] Matthew 3. 15.

[27] That is, Florence. See above § 1 and note 7.

[28] Lucan, *Pharsalia*, I. 280-82. Curio is graphically described in *Inferno* XXVIII, where he is punished by having his tongue cut out as a 'sower of schism': 'Questi

Anubis,[29] rebuking Aeneas, be heard again too: 'If the glory of your great destiny is powerless to kindle your ardour, and if you will exert no effort to win fame for yourself, at least think of Ascanius, now growing up, and all that you hope from him as your heir, destined to rule in an Italy which shall become the Italy of Rome.'[30]

[5] For your royal firstborn, John,[31] a king in his own right,[32] to whom, once the sun has set on the day which is now dawning,[33] the world's future generations will turn, is for us another Ascanius. Following in the footsteps of his great father, he will attack the followers of Turnus like a lion, wherever they may be,[34] but towards the followers of Latinus he will be as gentle as a lamb.[35] So let our divinely appointed king beware in his lofty judgement, lest divine justice speak out again with the bitter words of Samuel: 'Small as you may be in your own eyes, are you not head of the

---

[...] il dubitar sommerse | in Cesare, affermando che 'l fornito | sempre con danno l'attender sofferse' (*Inf.*, XXVIII. 97-99).

[29] Anubis is the jackal-headed Egyptian god of the dead. He was identified by the Romans with the god Mercury, who is, in fact, the speaker in the passage quoted from the *Aeneid*. Uguccione da Pisa makes this identification explicit: '**Anubis** [...], idest Mercurius' [**Anubis**, that is, Mercury] (*Derivationes*, II. 854).

[30] *Aeneid*, IV. 272-76.

[31] John of Luxembourg, the son of Henry VII, was born in 1296 and was killed at the battle of Crécy in 1346.

[32] John had become King of Bohemia in 1310 by virtue of his marriage to Elizabeth, the sister of the murdered King Wenceslas III.

[33] That is, after the death of Henry VII. John was never to succeed his father; and, in fact, Dante seems conveniently to forget here that the title of Holy Roman Emperor was, at this time, decided by election, not by right of heredity.

[34] In the *Aeneid*, Turnus, the king of the Rutulians, opposes Aeneas and fights him for control of Italy. The 'followers of Turnus' therefore implies all those who oppose the Empire. The comparison with a lion here recalls Virgil's description of Mezentius, one of the supporters of Turnus, in book X of the *Aeneid*: 'as many a time some ravenous lion wandering among fenced cattle-farms urged by a frantic hunger, chancing to see a fleeting goat or a stag with towering antlers, rejoices, and monstrously gaping, with bristling mane, he lies at his feast over his victim, clinging to its entrails, while gruesomely the blood bathes the unpitying jaws; such now was the agile onslaught of Mezentius against his serried foes' (*Aeneid*, X. 723-29). Significantly, in this context, Mezentius is killed by Aeneas.

[35] The followers of Latinus supported Aeneas in his battle against Turnus. The term here is therefore used to refer to those people who support the Empire.

tribes of Israel? Yahweh has anointed you king over Israel. Yahweh sent you on a mission and said to you, "Go, put these sinners, the Amalekites, under the ban and make war on them until they are exterminated".'[36] For you too have been anointed king in order to kill Amalek and not spare Agag;[37] and you must exact the vengeance of the one who sent you on that 'brutal people' and their 'premature rejoicing' (for this is what the names 'Amalek' and 'Agag' are said to connote).

[6] Do you intend to linger in Milan throughout the spring as you have done through the winter,[38] supposing that you will be able to kill the pestilent hydra simply by chopping off its heads? If you were to cast your mind over the great deeds of the glorious Alcides,[39] you would realize that you had fallen into the same error as him; for the deadly beast grew stronger with each blow against it, as each head sprouted into many more, until the hero struck with all his might at the very source of its life.[40] To fell a tree, there is no point simply cutting off its branches, for this will only make far more new branches grow more strongly than before, as long as the roots remain undamaged in order to provide it with nutrients. Sole ruler of the world, what do you think you will achieve by crushing

---

[36] I Samuel 15. 17-18. Samuel is here criticizing Saul for not having followed God's orders to the letter. Rather than kill all the Amalekites and destroy their property, Saul had spared the Amalekite king, Agag, and had saved the best of his sheep, cattle and produce to offer to God in sacrifice.

[37] Agag is eventually killed by Samuel (I Samuel 15. 33).

[38] Henry stayed at Milan from 23 December 1310 until 19 April 1311, two days after the date of this letter.

[39] Alcides is an alternative name for Hercules. The slaying of the Lernaean hydra – a monstrous and many-headed beast – constituted the second of his twelve labours. The task was rendered near-impossible by the fact that, whenever one of the hydra's heads was chopped off, two more grew in its place, and by the fact that one of the heads was immortal: 'The hydra throve on its wounds, and none of its hundred heads could be cut off with impunity, without being replaced by two new ones which made its neck stronger than ever' (Ovid, *Metamorphoses*, IX. 70-72). Eventually, Hercules was able to overcome the beast with the help of his nephew Iolaus. As soon as Hercules removed one of the beast's heads, Iolaus held a torch to the headless neck, cauterizing the wound and preventing the re-growth of more heads. Once all the other heads had been removed, the immortal head could also be amputated, at which point the hydra finally died. See Ovid, *Metamorphoses*, IX. 69-74.

[40] That is, the final, immortal head.

obstinate Cremona?[41] Will you prevent this unforeseen rebellion from spreading to Brescia or to Pavia?[42] In fact, no sooner will it have been beaten into submission there, than another will break out in Vercelli, or Bergamo, or elsewhere,[43] until the root cause of this contagion is eradicated. Only when the root of the problem has been pulled up, will the trunk and prickly branches wither.

[7] Do you not realize, most excellent prince, have you risen so high, your Highness,[44] that you cannot see where it is that this stinking vixen has gone to earth, safe from the hunters? It is not, to be sure, from the swift waters of the Po, nor from your own Tiber that this troublemaker drinks. Rather, her snarling jaws continue to pollute the rushing course of the Arno, and – did you really not know it? – Florence is the name of this ill-omened beast. She is the viper who turns against the vitals of her own mother;[45] she is the sick sheep, which infects her master's flock with her disease; she is Myrrha, wicked and ungodly, yearning for the embrace of her father, Cinyras;[46] she is the wrathful Amata, who refused to accept

---

[41] At Florence's instigation, Cremona had rebelled against Henry in February 1311. Henry entered the city and crushed the rebellion on 26 April.

[42] Like Cremona, Brescia rebelled against Henry in February 1311. The city was besieged by Henry's armies from 19 May until 19 September of the same year, and was eventually conquered by him, despite heavy losses on the imperial side (not least due to an outbreak of plague in the imperial camp). Opposition to Henry was also strong in Pavia, which he managed to pacify in October 1311, on his way from Brescia to Genoa.

[43] Vercelli, to the south-west of Milan, and Bergamo, to the north-east, represent the extent of Dante's Lombardy. Thus Dante is here predicting widespread uprising against Henry across the area previously loyal to him.

[44] There seems to be a play on words here. In Late Latin 'Celsitudo' was a term of respect, similar to 'Your Highness'. Here, however, the term seems to be used literally to suggest a high or lofty place, where a lookout post might be situated.

[45] There is a clear echo here of Anchises' condemnation of civil war, in the episode in *Aeneid* VI when he reveals his descendents to Aeneas in the Elysian Fields: 'Ah, sons of mine, never inure your spirits to so wicked a war [as that between Caesar and Pompey], never turn the stout strength of your homeland on her own vitals' (*Aeneid*, VI. 832-33).

[46] Dante would have been familiar with the story of Myrrha from Ovid's *Metamorphoses* (X. 298-518). Myrrha, the daughter of Cinyras, King of Cyprus, lusted after her own father, and eventually managed to sleep with him, disguised as another woman and under cover of darkness. When he discovered what he had done, her father chased her away with his sword, and she was turned into the myrrh tree. The son of her union with her father, Adonis, was born from the tree

the marriage ordained by fate and did not hesitate to choose as her son-in-law the suitor whom the gods rejected, sending him recklessly into war and finally, in recompense for the evil which she had dared to do, hanging herself.[47] With all the ferocity of a viper she strives to tear her mother to pieces, as she sharpens the horns of her rebellion against Rome, which made her in its own image and likeness.[48] She gives off fetid fumes, dripping with gore, which cause any nearby flocks still unaware of her ways to waste away, when, seducing them with insincere flattery and outright lies she wins her neighbours over to her side and, having won them over, makes fools of them. She burns with incestuous desire for her own father, when with wicked shamelessness she tries to violate the consensus between you and the supreme Pontiff, who is the father of fathers.[49] Truly she 'is rebelling against God's

---

nine months later. Myrrha is condemned by Dante in the tenth bolgia of the eighth circle of Hell for 'falsification of the person': 'Quell'è l'anima antica | di Mirra scellerata, che divenne | al padre, fuor del dritto amore, amica' (*Inf.*, XXX. 37-39).

[47] In the *Aeneid*, Amata was the wife of King Latinus and mother of Lavinia, whom the gods had chosen as the future wife of Aeneas. Amata, however, wished her daughter to marry Turnus, the King of the Rutulians and Aeneas's enemy, to whom Lavinia had originally been promised in marriage by Latinus. Believing that Turnus had been killed in battle against Aeneas, Amata hanged herself rather than see her daughter married to Aeneas. See *Aeneid*, VII. 341-72 and XII. 593-603, and compare the reference to the conflict between the Rutulians and the Latins in § 5 above. Amata is therefore presented here as someone who seeks to stand in the way of the divinely ordained establishment of the Roman Empire under Aeneas. In the *Purgatorio*, she is presented as an example of the sin of Wrath (*Purg.*, XVII. 35-39). Her hanging recalls that of Judas, whose death is described in the Vulgate in identical terms to those used here of Amata (Matthew 27. 5). It is clear from the description of the punishment of Brutus and Cassius alongside Judas in the mouths of Lucifer, that for Dante betrayal of the Empire is tantamount to Judas's betrayal of Christ.

[48] Compare Genesis 1. 26: 'God said: "Let us make man in our own image, in the likeness of ourselves".' This is probably intended by Dante to remind his readers that, after its destruction by Totila, Florence had been rebuilt on the model of Rome: 'La città nuova di Firenze si cominciò a redificare per gli Romani [...] di piccolo sito e giro, figurandola al modo di Roma, secondo la piccola impresa' (Villani, *Nuova cronica*, III. 2). Compare Dante's description of Florence, in the *Convivio*, as 'la bellissima e famosissima figlia di Roma' (*Conv.*, I. iii. 4).

[49] In trying to seduce the Pope – Clement V, who had initially been a supporter of Henry VII – away from the Emperor, Florence therefore behaves like the incestuous Myrrha, for the Pope is the father of all. Furthermore, it is implied that she thereby rejects her true husband; that is, Henry himself.

decision',[50] worshipping the idol of her own free will, when, having rejected the legitimate king, she is not ashamed, insane as she is, to barter rights which are not hers with a king who is not hers in order to have the power to do evil. But this madwoman should consider the noose in which she is binding herself. For it often happens that people are left to their own depraved devices, in order that, in their depravity, they do those things which should not be done.[51] Although such actions may be unjust, they may however be considered just if seen in terms of punishments.

[8] Arise then, and cease delaying, new son of Jesse.[52] Draw strength from the eyes of the Lord God of Hosts,[53] in whose sight you act, and cast down this Goliath with the sling of your wisdom and the stone of your strength, for with his defeat night and the shadow of fear will fall over the Philistine camp, the Philistines will flee, and Israel will be free.[54] Then our inheritance,[55] whose loss we unceasingly lament, will be fully restored to us. And even as we now sigh in our Babylonian exile when we remember the holy Jerusalem,[56] so then, restored to citizenship and breathing in

---

[50] Romans 13. 2. The same passage is quoted in letter V. 4.

[51] See Romans 1. 28: 'since they refused to see it was rational to acknowledge God, God has left them to their own irrational ideas and to their monstrous behaviour' (or, more literally, '[...] God gave them over to a depraved mind and to do those things which are not proper').

[52] Henry is here being compared to King David, who is frequently referred to as the 'son of Jesse' in many biblical contexts. See, for example, I Samuel 16. 18; I Samuel 20. 31; II Samuel 20. 1; I Kings 12. 16; I Chronicles 29. 26; Luke 3. 32. Even more significantly, in the *Convivio* the divinely preordained destinies of David and of Rome are bound up together: 'E tutto questo fu in uno temporale, che David nacque e nacque Roma, cioè che Enea venne di Troia in Italia, che fu origine de la cittade romana, sì come testimoniano le scritture. Per che assai è manifesto la divina elezione del romano imperio, per lo nascimento de la santa cittade che fu contemporaneo a la radice de la progenie di Maria' (*Conv.*, IV. v. 6).

[53] The Latin formulation used here 'Domini Dei Sabaoth' is also strongly biblical.

[54] Here the comparison with David is continued, therefore, and Florence is equated with David's legendary adversary, Goliath. See I Samuel 17. 1-54.

[55] That is, the peace which, according to the first sentence of this letter, was God's bequest to humanity.

[56] Compare Psalm 136 [137]. 1: 'Beside the streams of Babylon we sat and wept at the memory of Zion', and see § 1 and note 6, above.

peace, will we remember in our joy the miseries of our time of confusion.

Written on 17 April, in Tuscany, beneath the source of the Arno, in the first year of the Emperor Henry's most auspicious descent into Italy.[57]

---

[57] Compare the closing paragraph of letter VI, written in the same place only eighteen days earlier. Compare also the closing words of letter X, in which the castle of Poppi is explicitly named. The 'first year of Henry's descent into Italy' is, as before, 1311.

The Letter to the Italian Cardinals (Letter XI)

Introduction: Spring 1314

Pope Clement V died on 20 April 1314. He had been elected to the papacy in June 1305, after a fraught conclave, held at Perugia, which had lasted ten months. The cardinals had been split, with Matteo Orsini and Francesco Caetani leading one faction (roughly speaking, the 'Italian' faction), which supported the memory and policies of Boniface VIII, and Napoleone Orsini leading the other faction, which allied itself with the French cardinals' opposition to Boniface and his policies. At Perugia, the 'French' faction proved stronger, and Bertrand de Got, archbishop of Bordeaux, was elected as Pope Clement V, initiating what Dante presents as the institution's 'Babylonian' exile in Avignon.

With Clement's death, Dante was anxious to see the mistakes made at the conclave of Perugia reversed. Sometime in May or June 1314,[1] he wrote to the cardinals gathered at Carpentras, and specifically to the Italians among them, urging them to elect a Pope who would restore the Papacy to its rightful place in Rome. He laments the state of contemporary Rome, 'deprived of both her lights, whom now Hannibal himself [...] should pity, [...] lonely and widowed' (XI. 10), and attacks the clergy for having abandoned the works of the Church Fathers in favour of those works of Canon Law which enable them to increase their temporal power, while leaving their flocks to go astray, leading them 'to the very edge of the precipice' (XI. 4). Dante attacks representatives of both the 'Italian' and the 'French' factions at the Perugia conclave, but in particular Napoleone Orsini, insisting on the danger of allowing political wrangling to obstruct the choice of a spiritual leader.

As in the case of his letters concerning Henry VII, however, Dante's words were to fall on deaf ears. On 14 July 1314, the conclave at Carpentras was violently broken up by supporters of the 'French' faction and the Italian cardinals were forced to flee. The Papacy remained vacant for more than two years, until finally the conclave was reconvened at Lyon and Pope John XXII was

---

[1] On the dating of this letter, see Toynbee, *Epistolae*, pp. 124-26.

elected on 7 August 1316. The Papacy remained at Avignon until 1377.

Letter XI[1]

[1] 'Oh how lonely she sits, the city once thronged with people. She who was great among the nations has become like a widow'.[2] At one time, the cupidity of the princes of the Pharisees,[3] which so corrupted the ancient priesthood, not only excluded the children of Levi from their ministry,[4] but also brought siege and destruction down upon the chosen city of David.[5] And when he who alone is

---

[1] This letter lacks the formal introductory statement naming writer and addressee found in the previous three letters translated here. Printed editions of the letter traditionally give it with the heading 'Cardinalibus ytalicis Dantes de Florentia, etc.' (To the Italian Cardinals, from Dante the Florentine, etc.).

[2] Lamentations 1. 1. This verse is also quoted by Dante in the *Vita nuova* (XXVIII. 1), where it marks the death of Beatrice, and where its use is explained as follows: 'Poi che fue partita da questo secolo, rimase tutta la sopradetta cittade quasi vedova dispogliata da ogni dignitade; onde io, ancora lagrimando in questa desolata cittade, scrissi a li principi de la terra alquanto de la sua condizione, pigliando quello cominciamento di Geremia profeta che dice: "*Quomodo sedet sola civitas*"' (*VN*, XXX. 1). The letter to the 'princes of the earth' (or perhaps just the 'rulers of the city'), if indeed it really existed, has not survived; however, the repetition of this quotation suggests that Dante may date the beginning of Florence's (and, by extension, Italy's) decline from the death of Beatrice. The relevance of this passage to Dante's view of contemporary Italy is attested also by the echoes of it which can be found in the invective against Italy of *Purgatorio* VI ('non donna di province', line 78; Roma che piagne | vedova e sola', lines 112-13). The translation of the biblical passage used here is adapted from that of the Jerusalem Bible, which punctuates the passage differently.

[3] In *Inferno*, XXVII. 85, in the encounter with Guido da Montefeltro, Boniface VIII is described as 'Lo principe d'i novi Farisei'.

[4] 'The Levites [...] came to Judah and Jerusalem, since Jeroboam and his sons had excluded them from the priesthood of Yahweh, and had set up for himself a priesthood of the high places, for the satyrs and the calves he had made' (II Chronicles 11. 14-15). Jeroboam became king of the northern kingdom of Israel after the death of Solomon, and deliberately provoked division between his kingdom, with its capital at Shechem, and the kingdom of Judah, whose capital was Jerusalem. Appointing priests who were not Levites, he encouraged his people to the idolatrous worship of two golden calves, seen as symbols of God. The political and religious division effected by Jeroboam, and his displacement of the centre of religious authority from the Temple in Jerusalem to the golden calves at Bethel and Dan, is clearly seen as prefiguring the political and religious disorder caused by the papacy's involvement in secular affairs in Dante's time, and in particular the removal of the seat of the papacy to Avignon.

[5] That is, Jerusalem. At the end of letter VII, Henry VII is referred to as a 'second David', bringing together the destinies of Jerusalem and of Rome, as is seen also in *Convivio*, IV. v. 6 (see note 52 to letter VII in the present edition).

eternal, beheld this from his watchtower at the very tip of eternity,[6] he – through his Holy Spirit – impressed his command upon the mind (a mind worthy of God) of the prophet,[7] who, in the words written above – and repeated, alas, all too often –, wept for the holy city of Jerusalem, a city on the verge of destruction.

[2] For us men and for our salvation,[8] after his love had been questioned three times, Peter was told to feed the holy sheepfold;[9] that is, the city of Rome, which, after so much pomp and glory, was confirmed in its world-rule by the words and deeds of Christ,[10] and which was consecrated as the Apostolic See by Peter himself and by Paul, the Apostle to the Gentiles,[11] through the shedding of their own blood. Yet now, we – who believe that Father and Son, God and Man, Mother and Virgin are one and the same – we too, like Jeremiah, find ourselves compelled to weep for our own widowed, lonely city; not in anticipation of things to come, but rather in suffering after the event.

---

[6] The manuscript is unclear at this point (as at several others in this letter) leading to variations in the translation of this passage. Frugoni's edition – which my translation follows – reads 'de specula punctalis eternitatis', whereas Toynbee prefers the reading 'de specula punctali aeternitatis' (translated as 'from his eternal watch-tower on high'). In support of his conviction that 'punctalis' must agree with 'eternitatis', Frugoni cites *Paradiso*, XVII. 17-18, where Cacciaguida is portrayed gazing into the eternal present of God's mind: 'mirando il punto | a cui tutti li tempi son presenti'.

[7] That is, Jeremiah.

[8] The wording here is reminiscent of the Nicene Creed, which refers to Christ 'who, for us men and for our salvation, came down from Heaven'.

[9] This is a reference to the account, in St John's Gospel, of Christ's final appearance to his disciples on the shores of the Sea of Galilee: 'After the meal, Jesus said to Simon Peter, "Simon, son of John, do you love me more than these others do?". He answered, "Yes Lord, you know I love you". Jesus said to him, "Feed my lambs". A second time he said to him, "Simon, son of John, do you love me?". He replied, "Yes, Lord, you know I love you". Jesus said to him, "Look after my sheep". Then he said to him a third time, "Simon, son of John, do you love me?". Peter was upset that he asked him the third time, "Do you love me?" and said, "Lord, you know everything; you know I love you". Jesus said to him, "Feed my sheep" ' (John, 21. 15-17). This passage is followed by a prediction of Peter's violent death.

[10] See letter V. 9-10; letter VI. 1; letter VII. 3.

[11] Compare Romans 11. 13.

[3] Alas, the sight of this lamentable[12] wound saddens us no less than the fact that those people who instigate immoral heresies[13] – Jews, Saracens, and Gentiles[14] – mock our Sabbaths[15] and, so it is said, cry out, 'Where is their God?'.[16] It saddens us still more that those fallen angels who resist the angelic guardians may perhaps attribute this work to their own treachery;[17] and – what is worse – that various star-gazers and ignorant fortune-tellers assert that certain things happened out of divine predestination, when in fact you brought them about of your own misguided, free will.[18]

[4] Indeed, you, who lead the Church Militant as its highest-ranking soldiers,[19] have gone off course, just like the false

---

[12] Dante's use of the adjective *lamentabilis* ('deserving or arousing lamentation') is clearly intended as a reference back to the Lamentations of Jeremiah, which have been a constant point of reference throughout §§ 1 and 2 of this letter. This has been conveyed in translation through the use of the word 'lamentable', even though in modern English the term more often conveys a sense of moral disapproval which is absent here.

[13] I follow Frugoni's reading of this passage (which is unclear in the manuscript). Toynbee makes 'heresies' refer back to 'plagam lamentabilem': 'the lamentable plague of heresies'.

[14] Dante seems, in this phrase, to be pointing to the fact that Rome, and Rome's divinely willed destiny, is under attack from all sides: not just from the traditional enemies of Christianity, but also from within.

[15] This phrase (in Dante's Latin, 'sabbata nostra rident') seems to take up the earlier references to the book of Lamentations. In the Vulgate, Lamentations 1. 7 concludes, 'et deriserunt sabbata eius', which is variously translated either as 'they mocked her ruin' or 'downfall' or as 'they mocked her sabbaths'.

[16] See Psalm 78 [79]. 10: 'Why should the pagans ask, "Where is their God" '.

[17] Compare Ephesians 6. 11-12: 'Put God's armour on so as to be able to resist the devil's tactics. For it is not against human enemies that we have to struggle, but against the Sovereignties and the Powers who originate the darkness in this world, the spiritual army of evil in the heavens'.

[18] Here Dante addresses the cardinals directly for the first time. Until this point, he has used the first person plural form, expressing the point of view of the 'lamenter'. It is only here that he turns to address the cardinals (and, with them, the cause of the dire situation outlined in the letter's first two paragraphs) directly and to begin to identify a cause for the present political and religious disorder.

[19] Dante's reference here is to the *primipilus*, the most senior centurion in a Roman legion. Significantly, in terms of the imagery of empire habitually used by Dante, the sacred Eagle of the legion was normally entrusted to the *primipilus*. See also *Paradiso*, XXIV. 59, where Dante-Pilgrim describes St Peter as 'l'alto primipilo' during his examination on Faith. The Pilgrim goes on, in a way which

charioteer Phaeton,[20] neglecting to steer the chariot of the Bride of Christ along the path revealed to you. You, whose duty it was to light the way of your faithful flock through the wood of this earthly pilgrimage, have led your followers and yourselves to the very edge of the precipice.[21] Nor, since you keep your backs rather than your faces turned towards the Bride's chariot (so that you might justifiably be compared to the men who were shown to the prophet Ezekiel with their backs turned to the Temple[22]), do I see the need to provide examples to illustrate this for you: you, who scorn the

---

recalls § 2 of the present letter, to refer also to St Paul and to his role, alongside Peter, in bringing Christianity to Rome: 'tuo caro frate | che mise teco Roma nel buon filo' (*Par.*, XXIV. 62-63).

[20] Phaeton, according to the very famous legend (known to Dante from *Metamorphoses*, II. 1-332), was the son of the sun-god, Apollo (also referred to as Phoebus). As proof of his devotion to his son, Apollo reluctantly agrees to allow Phaeton to drive his chariot (the sun) across the sky for a day. Phaeton loses control of the sun's horses, scorches parts of the earth to permanent desert, and is eventually struck down by Jupiter's thunderbolts, at the urging of the goddess of the earth who fears complete destruction. Dante refers to this legend on various occasions in the *Commedia*, as for example in *Inferno*, XVII. 106-07 to convey the fear that his pilgrim feels on the back of the monstrous Geryon ('Maggior paura non credo che fosse, | quando Fetòn abbandonò li freni'), in *Purgatorio*, IV. 71-72 and *Paradiso*, XXXI. 124-25 to convey the passage of the sun across the sky ('la strada | che mal non seppe carreggiar Feton'; 'il temo | che mal guidò Fetonte') and, perhaps most famously, in *Paradiso*, XVII. 1-3, where the pilgrim's anxiety to know the truth about the prophecies which have been made about him during the course of his journey is compared to Phaeton's desire to know the truth about his parentage.

[21] The mention of the wood and the lost path here cannot but recall the opening lines of the *Commedia*: 'mi ritrovai per una selva oscura | ché la diritta via era smarrita' (*Inf.*, I. 2-3). The emphasis on the lack of proper guidance on the part of Church leaders also recalls *Convivio*, IV. xxiv. 12: 'così l'adolescente, che entra ne la selva erronea di questa vita, non saprebbe tenere lo buono cammino, se da li suoi maggiori non li fosse mostrato'.

[22] The name Ezekiel has been added to the translation, to clarify that 'the prophet' referred to here is no longer Jeremiah, who has been a major point of reference in §§ 1-3. The passage refers to Ezekiel's vision of the sins of Jerusalem: 'He then led me to the inner court of the Temple of Yahweh. And there, at the entrance to the sanctuary of Yahweh, between the porch and the altar, there were about twenty-five men, with their backs to the sanctuary of Yahweh and their faces turned to the east. They were bowing to the east, towards the sun' (Ezekiel 8. 16). The reference to sun-worship here seems to take up Dante's earlier reference to Phaeton.

flames that fall from heaven,[23] while now the altars are alight with unlawful fire;[24] you who sell pigeons in the Temple,[25] while those things whose value cannot be measured are made available for a price, to the detriment of both buyers and sellers. But beware of the whip, beware of the fire and do not take for granted the patience of God, which is meant to lead you to repentance.[26] And if you are in any doubt about that precipice which I mentioned, what else can I say by way of explanation, except that you have behaved like Demetrius when he agreed to the appointment of Alcimus.[27]

[5] Will you, perhaps, reproach me indignantly, asking 'who is this who does not fear the sudden punishment of Uzzah, but sets himself up as the protector of the Ark, no matter how unsteady it

---

[23] This passage recalls the story of Elijah's sacrifice on Mount Carmel (I Kings 18. 20-40). Elijah assembles four hundred and fifty prophets of Baal and challenges them to call on their god to bring down fire onto the ritual sacrifice of a bull. The prophets of Baal 'took the bull and prepared it, and from morning to midday they called on the name of Baal. "O Baal, answer us!" they cried, but there was no voice, no answer'. When Elijah prepares his bull, however, 'the fire of Yahweh fell and consumed the holocaust and wood and licked up the water in the trench'.

[24] Another point of reference here seems to be the story of the 'unlawful' (the word used in the Vulgate is *alienus*, as in Dante's letter) fire of Nadab and Abihu: 'each took his censer, put fire in it and incense on the fire, and presented unlawful fire before Yahweh, fire which he had not prescribed for them. Then from Yahweh's presence a flame leaped out and consumed them, and they perished in the presence of Yahweh' (Leviticus 10. 1-2).

[25] 'Just before the Jewish Passover Jesus went up to Jerusalem, and in the Temple he found people selling cattle and sheep and pigeons, and the money changers sitting at their counters there. Making a whip out of some cord, he drove them all out of the Temple, cattle and sheep as well, scattered the money changers' coins, knocked their tables over and said to the pigeon-sellers, "Take all this out of here and stop turning my Father's house into a market" ' (John 2. 13-15). The passage also recalls the fact that in *Paradiso*, XVII. 51 Dante describes the court of Boniface VIII as 'là dove Cristo tutto dì si merca'.

[26] Compare Romans 2. 4: 'Or are you abusing his abundant goodness, patience and toleration, not realizing that this goodness of God is meant to lead you to repentance?'.

[27] 'The godless Alcimus' (I Maccabees 7. 9), a bitter enemy of Judas Maccabeus, persuaded King Demetrius I of Syria to appoint him as High Priest, a position which he then used to trick and to attempt to destroy the Israelites loyal to Judas. The reference here seems to be to the previous conclave, when Clement V was elected to the Papacy, under the improper influence of Philip the Fair of France.

may be?'.²⁸ I am, without doubt, the least of the sheep in the pasture of Jesus Christ, and certainly I am not taking advantage of any pastoral authority since I possess no wealth. It is, therefore, not thanks to riches but by the grace of God that I am what I am,²⁹ and 'zeal for his house devours me'.³⁰ For that truth which is pleasing to God proceeds even from the mouths of babes and sucklings,³¹ and a man born blind has proclaimed the truth that the Pharisees not only do not acknowledge, but rather maliciously contradict.³² These things give me the courage of my convictions. Besides, I also have the authority of Aristotle,³³ who, in setting out the principles of ethics, taught that truth is more important than friendship.³⁴ Nor am I sullied by stain of the sin of Uzzah, although some have thought to accuse me of similar presumption, as though I had spoken out rashly; for, whereas Uzzah reached out his hand to the Ark itself, I reach out to the recalcitrant oxen who are pulling

---

[28] 'When they came to the threshing-floor of Nacon, Uzzah stretched his hand out to the ark of God and steadied it, as the oxen were making it tilt. Then the anger of Yahweh blazed out against Uzzah, and for this crime God struck him down on the spot, and he died there beside the ark of God' (II Samuel 6. 6-7; and compare *Purgatorio*, X. 56-57). The previous paragraph's image of the chariot of the Church gone astray is taken up here in that of the unsteady progress of the Ark of the Covenant.

[29] 'I am the least of the apostles; in fact, since I persecuted the Church of God, I hardly deserve the name apostle; but by God's grace that is what I am' (I Corinthians XV. 9-10).

[30] Psalm 68. 10 [69. 9].

[31] Psalm 8. 3 [8. 2]

[32] John's Gospel tells the story of the cure of a man blind from birth, who, Jesus claims, 'was born blind so that the works of God might be displayed in him' (John 9. 2). Jesus's curing of the man on the Sabbath, however, is attacked by the Pharisees, who claim that 'this man cannot be from God: he does not keep the sabbath' (John 9. 16). The true vision of the blind man, who accepts Jesus as the Son of God (John 9. 38) is thus contrasted to the spiritual blindness of the Pharisees. From the beginning of this letter, moreover, the Pharisees have been identified with the corrupt leaders of the contemporary Church.

[33] In the original Latin, as elsewhere in Dante's works, Aristotle is referred to simply as 'the Philosopher'.

[34] 'Quello maestro de li filosofi, Aristotile, nel principio de l'Etica [...] dice: "Se due sono li amici, e uno è la verità, a la verità è da consentire" ' (*Conv.*, IV. viii. 15); and see *Ethics*, I. vi: 'for one might love both, but it is nevertheless a sacred duty to prefer the truth to one's friends'.

it off course.[35] I pray that God, who turned the salvific power of his gaze onto the little boat tossed by the waves,[36] will also come to the aid of the Ark.

[6] It would seem, then, that rather than having incited people to anger, I have provoked only blushes of confusion (if, that is, shame has not been utterly eradicated from the world) in you and in others, archimandrites in name only.[37] For among so many who usurp of the role of shepherd, and amidst so many sheep, neglected and uncared-for at pasture, if not actually driven away, just one voice, a lone voice of devotion – and the voice of a layman at that – can be heard, as if at the funeral of our mother, the Church.

[7] And this is not surprising. Just like you, all men have espoused cupidity – the cupidity from which spring immorality and unfairness, and never the morality and justice which come from charity.[38] Oh, most holy mother and bride of Christ! Through water and the Spirit,[39] you bear sons, who bring you only shame. Neither charity nor justice,[40] but the daughters of the leech[41] have become your daughters-in-law, and to see what kind of offspring they bear

---

[35] That is to say, Dante addresses his rebukes not against the Church itself but against the corrupt clergy who are leading it astray.

[36] See the story of Jesus's calming of the storm (Matthew 8. 23-27; Mark 4. 35-41; Luke 8. 22-25).

[37] The term 'archimandrite' refers, in modern usage, to the superior of a monastery or group of monasteries in the Eastern Orthodox tradition. Dante appears to have used the term to refer to any religious leader, since it is used of St Francis in *Paradiso*, XI. 99 and of St Peter in *Monarchia*, III. ix. 17. The term takes up the shepherd imagery found elsewhere in this letter, since it means, literally, 'one who rules the sheepfold'.

[38] Charity, or Christian love, is the virtue which opposes the sin of cupidity, to which Dante returns so frequently in these letters.

[39] See Jesus's exchange with Nicodemus: 'I tell you most solemnly, unless a man is born through water and the Spirit, he cannot enter the kingdom of God' (John 3. 5).

[40] In Dante's original Latin, Justice is indicated indirectly through a reference to the goddess Astrea. As Dante explains in *Monarchia*, I. xi. 1, in his explanation of the famous line from Virgil's *Eclogue* IV predicting the coming of a new Golden Age: ' "Now the Virgin returns, the reign of Saturn returns". For "the virgin" was their name for justice, whom they also called "Astrea" '. See also note 10 to letter VII.

[41] See Proverbs 30. 15: 'The leech has two daughters'.

you, it is enough to look at any one of them, with the exception of the Bishop of Luni.[42] Your beloved Gregory languishes in the cobwebs;[43] Ambrose lies neglected by the clergy in some forgotten corner,[44] along with Augustine,[45] Dionysius,[46] John Damascene,[47] and Bede.[48] Instead, they trumpet some *Speculum* or other, and the works of Innocent and the man from Ostia.[49] And this is only to be

---

[42] The reference here is to Gherardino Malaspina, bishop of Luni from 1312 to 1321. A committed Guelph and a friend of Clement V, the bishop refused to submit to Henry VII or to take part in his coronation in Milan, and was, as a result, stripped of his temporal powers. Given the bishop's opposition to Henry VII, Dante's exclusion of him from the condemnation of all the other clerics here can only be ironic, and is reminiscent of the condemnation of the barrators of Lucca in *Inferno* XXI: 'ognun v'è barattier, fuor che Bonturo' (*Inf.*, XXI. 41).

[43] Gregory the Great. Pope from 590 until 604, Gregory is often described as the 'father of the medieval Papacy', since he did much to establish the supreme authority of the Bishop of Rome over the Church as a whole. Very much in line with Dante's own views, he saw the Church and the Empire as clearly distinct authorities within the religious and secular spheres respectively.

[44] St Ambrose was Bishop of Milan from 374 until his death in 397. Renowned as a man of exceptional holiness, he was instrumental in the conversion of St Augustine.

[45] St Augustine of Hippo, 354-430. Having been converted from Manichaeanism, Augustine became one of the great Christian thinkers of the early Middle Ages. His best-known works are his *Confessions*, *The City of God*, and *On Christian Doctrine*.

[46] The reference here is to the figure now known as Pseudo-Dionysius, a Christian Neo-Platonist, writing in the late fifth or early sixth century. 'Pseudo-Dionysius' presented himself in his writings as Dionysius the Areopagite, mentioned as having been converted to Christianity by St Paul himself in Acts 17. 34, and this identity was accepted throughout the Middle Ages.

[47] St John Damascene was born in around 676 and died between 754 and 787. He is sometimes known as the last of Greek Fathers, and is famous for having defended the veneration of images.

[48] The Venerable Bede was born in 672 or 673 and died in 735. He was a Benedictine monk, based in Northumberland, and is best known for his *Ecclesiastical History of the English People*, which – bringing Dante's list of the great Christian figures of the past full-circle – contains a famous account of the life of Gregory the Great.

[49] The neglected works of the Church Fathers are juxtaposed with works focusing on the intricacies of Canon Law: the *Speculum iudiciale* of Wilhelmus Durandus, and the works of Innocent IV (pope from 1243 to 1254 and a learned canon lawyer, famous for his commentary on the *Decretals* of Gregory IX) and of Henry of Susa (cardinal-bishop of Ostia and another famous thirteenth-century

expected, for the former sought God as their goal and supreme good, whereas the latter pursue only wealth and favours.

[8] Do not, however, assume, Fathers, that I am unique in the world, like the phoenix.[50] In fact, everyone is murmuring or muttering or thinking or dreaming these same things which I am saying out loud, but they do not speak out about what they have seen. There are some people whose bewilderment makes them hesitate;[51] but can they remain silent forever and will they never bear witness to their Maker? The Lord lives, for he who moved the tongue of Balaam's ass, is also the Lord of the dumb animals of our own times.[52]

---

decretalist). This sentence recalls several of the passages of anti-clerical invective in the *Commedia*; in particular, *Paradiso*, IX. 133-35 ('Per questo l'Evangelio e i dottor magni | son derelitti, e solo ai Decretali | si studia') and *Paradiso*, XII. 82-85, in reference to St Dominic: 'Non per lo mondo, per cui mo s'affanna | di retro ad Ostïense e a Taddeo, | ma per amor de la verace manna | in picciol tempo gran dottor si feo.'

[50] According to mythology, supported by medieval bestiaries, there was only one phoenix, which was reborn every five hundred year from its own ashes. Brunetto Latini, for example, writes that the phoenix is: 'uns oiseaus en Arrabe dont il n'a plus que un sol en trestout le monde' (*Tresor*, I. 164). See also *Inferno*, XXIV. 106-11.

[51] Dante literally states here that these people are 'suspended' in bewilderment, recalling Virgil's famous description of the souls in Limbo as 'color che son sospesi' (*Inf.*, II. 52).

[52] Balaam was a prophet or soothsayer, employed by the Moabite king, Balak, to curse the Israelites in the hope of preventing defeat by them in battle. Despite repeated warnings from God not to carry out the curse, Balaam sets out with the intention of doing as Balak had requested. Twice an angel blocks Balaam's way and forces his donkey off the path, and each time Balaam beats the donkey mercilessly. On the third occasion that the angel blocks the way, the donkey is completely unable to pass, and lies down on the path, receiving yet another beating. 'Then Yahweh opened the mouth of the donkey, who said to Balaam: "What have I done to you? Why beat me three times like this?" Balaam answered the donkey, "Because you are playing the fool with me! If I had a sword in my hand, I would have killed you by now." The donkey said to Balaam, "Am I not your donkey, and have I not been your mount from your youth? In all this time, have I ever failed to serve you?" He answered, "No". Then Yahweh opened the eyes of Balaam. He saw the angel of the Yahweh standing on the road, a drawn sword in his hand; and he bowed down and fell prostrate on his face' (Numbers 22. 28-31). In this case, Dante is clearly casting himself in the role of the donkey, the humble and faithful servant who is, despite its low status, able to see the truth to which its master is blind. He also takes on, however, something of the prophetic

[9] Now I have become talkative; but you have forced me into it.[53] You should be ashamed, therefore, at being condemned and rebuked by such a humble person, rather than by the Heavens, to which you should turn for forgiveness. For it is only right that we should be taken to task in such a way that shame is able to pervade our hearing, as well as our other senses, so that this shame gives birth in us to her firstborn, repentance, which in turn begets the resolution to make amends.

[10] And in order that this resolution be nurtured and protected by glorious forbearance, you should bear in mind, as far as your imagination allows, the condition of the city of Rome, now deprived of both her lights,[54] whom now Hannibal himself,[55] let alone anyone else, should pity,[56] who sits lonely and widowed, as is proclaimed above. And these things are especially pertinent to those of you who have known the sacred Tiber[57] since childhood. For although all Italians should love their capital city dutifully, as the foundation of their shared civilization,[58] it is rightly felt that

---

quality of Balaam himself, the outsider who nonetheless is inspired by God to see, and eventually to speak, the truth.

[53] Compare II Corinthians 12. 11: 'I have been talking like a fool, but you forced me to do it.'

[54] The two lights here, as in previous letters, represent the Emperor and the Pope (see letter V. 10 and note 47 in this edition; letter VI. 2, and compare *Monarchia*, III. iv. At the time of writing this letter, Rome is deprived of both: the Papacy is vacant following the death of Clement V, and the Empire has been contested between Louis of Bavaria and Frederick of Austria since the death of Henry VII in 1313. Compare *Purgatorio*, XVI. 106-08, where the two powers are, significantly, referred to as two suns, rather than as the sun and the moon, indicating Dante's view of them as equal, but separate, authorities.

[55] A reference to the great Carthaginian General and enemy of Rome, famous in particular for having marched a full army (including elephants) across the Alps and into Italy at the outbreak of the Second Punic War.

[56] This phrase recalls the description of Italy in letter V as 'you, whom now even the Saracens should pity' (V. 2), and is quoted, almost verbatim, by Petrarch in his *canzone* 53, 'Spirto gentil': 'ch'Anibale, non ch'altri, farian pio' (line 65).

[57] See *Aeneid*, VIII. 72: 'Father Tiber, you, and your hallowed stream, receive me, Aeneas.' Here, the Tiber stands synecdochically for the whole city of Rome.

[58] Clearly the use of the term 'Italian' with reference to this period is anomalous, and should not be taken as suggesting that Dante had any concept of 'Italy' as a political entity. It is clear from the *De vulgari eloquentia*, however, that he does believe that the inhabitants of the Italian peninsula are linked by a *cultural* bond,

you should show it special devotion, since for you it is the foundation of your very being. And if the wretchedness of the present time has overwhelmed all other Italians with sorrow and troubled them with shame, who could doubt that you, who were the cause of this unprecedented eclipse of Rome's Sun, should blush and grieve?[59] You, first and foremost, Orsini,[60] because of your intervention in favour of your disgraced colleagues, so that they should not remain forever without the glory of their office,[61] and so that, by the highest apostolic authority, they should be allowed to take up again the insignia of the Church Militant, insignia which they may not have deserved to bear, but which they had been forced, undeservedly, to lay down.[62] And you too, from across the

---

epitomized by the shared *volgare illustre* which that work attempts to define, a language which 'has left its scent in every city but made its home in none' (*DVE*, I. xvi. 4). Likewise, Dante clarifies that Italy may not be a unified kingdom, but it does not lack a 'court', however scattered this may be: 'although it is true that there is no such tribunal in Italy – in the sense of single institution, like that of the king of Germany – yet its constituent elements are not lacking. And just as the elements of the German tribunal are united under a single monarch, so those of the Italian have been brought together by the gracious light of reason. So it would not be true to say that the Italians lack a tribunal altogether, even though we lack a monarch, because we do have one, but its physical components are scattered' (*DVE*, I. xviii. 5).

[59] The 'eclipse' of Rome's sun (the Papacy) can be dated from the election of Clement V and the Papacy's subsequent removal to Avignon. The Italian cardinals named here are blamed for their support, at the time of the Perugia conclave, for Clement's election, which had – as Dante makes clear – purely personal motivations.

[60] Napoleone Orsini, had been made a cardinal in 1288 and was a brother of Pope Nicolas III. Napoleone had supported the election of Clement V, against the rest of the Orsini family, although in the Carpentras conclave he opposed the French faction, in the hope of electing an Italian (or pro-Italian) pope. In the Latin of Dante's letter, Cardinal Orsini is referred to as 'Urse', 'Bear'. In fact, members of the Orsini family habitually referred to themselves as *filii ursi* or 'sons of the bear', as is seen also in Dante's account of his pilgrim's meeting with Nicholas III in Hell: 'fui figliuol dell'orsa' (*Inf.*, XIX. 70).

[61] This is a reference to Jacopo and Pietro Colonna, who had had the office of Cardinal taken from them in 1297 by Boniface VIII, with whose family the Colonnas were in conflict. They had been restored as Cardinals by Clement V in 1306 after Napoleone Orsini had helped to engineer his election.

[62] That is, their own behaviour may not have justified their elevation to the college of cardinals, and yet neither did they deserve to be stripped of their office by Boniface because of what was a purely political and personal feud.

Tiber, you who supported the other faction,[63] in whom the anger of the dead Pope put forth new shoots, like a branch grafted onto a trunk which is not its own,[64] that anger at defeated Carthage which you had not yet left behind, you could, in all conscience, put this intention before the country of the illustrious Scipios.

[11] Amends certainly will be made – although the mark of corruption will necessarily disfigure the Apostolic See until the fire for which the present heaven and earth are destined[65] – if all those of you, who were the authors of this transgression,[66] will now go forth together to fight bravely for the Bride of Christ, for the Seat of the Bride which is Rome, for our Italy and, in more general terms, for the whole of the City of God on pilgrimage in this life.[67] Then from the stadium where this contest has already begun,[68] with

---

[63] This seems to be a reference to Iacopo Stefaneschi, whose family owned land in Trastevere. He represents the pro-Boniface VIII faction, which had opposed the election of Clement V at Perugia. A different view is put forward by Toynbee, who reads this reference as being to the whole pro-Boniface Guelph party, whose headquarters were in Trastevere. In either case, Dante is here highlighting the political wrangling which lay behind the election of Clement V (and which he does not wish to see repeated at Carpentras in the election of the new Pope).

[64] The 'dead Pope' in this case is Boniface VIII, whose feuds were carried forward at the Perugia conclave by Stefaneschi and his faction.

[65] This is a reference to the Day of Judgement. See II Peter 3. 7: 'By by the same word the present sky and earth are destined for fire, and are only being reserved until Judgement Day so that all sinners may be destroyed.'

[66] That is, the election of Clement V.

[67] This is an Augustinian term. Augustine's 'City of God' exists in its perfect form only in Heaven, whereas the 'City of Man' which opposes the City of God is wholly corrupt and this-worldly. However, Christians on earth are seen as living *within* the City of Man, but not as part of it. Rather, they are already, ideally, citizens of the City of God, merely passing through the City of Man as pilgrims. Discussing the need for earthly, political peace, for instance, Augustine writes that 'the Heavenly City – *or rather that part of it which is on pilgrimage in this condition of mortality*, and which lives on the basis of faith – must needs make use of this peace also, until this mortal state, for which this kind of peace is essential, passes away. And, therefore, it leads what we may call a life of captivity in this earthly city as in a foreign land' (*City of God*, XIX. 17; my italics).

[68] That is, the conclave which has already begun at Carpentras, to which the whole of Christendom is looking for leadership, guidance and – in Dante's view – for a return to Rome. The image recalls that used by St Paul in I Corinthians 9. 24-26: 'All the runners at the stadium are trying to win, but only one of them gets the prize. You must run in the same way, meaning to win. All the fighters at the

the eyes of the world upon you even from the furthest reaches of the ocean, you may offer yourselves up with glory, in order to hear 'Gloria in excelsis',[69] and the disgrace of the Gascons,[70] who, aflame with so much ill-omened cupidity, strive to usurp for themselves the glory of the Italians, may be held up as an example for posterity for centuries to come.

---

games go into strict training; they do this just to win a wreath that will wither away, but we do it for a wreath that will never wither'.

[69] See the description of Christ's triumphal entry into Jerusalem: 'They cried out "Blessings on the King who comes, in the name of the Lord! Peace in heaven and glory in the highest heavens"' (Luke 19. 38). Dante would therefore seem to be drawing a parallel here between Christ's entry into Jerusalem and the next Pope's imagined return to Rome.

[70] That is, the French cardinals, the supporters of Clement V and of a continuation of the Avignon Papacy, as against a return to Rome.

Bibliography

Primary Sources

Albertus Magnus, *De natura loci*, ed. by Paul Hossfeld, in *Opera omnia*, 37 vols (Aschendorff: Monasterii Westfalorum, 1955-), vol. V. ii

Aristotle, *Nicomachean Ethics*, trans. by Roger Crisp (Cambridge: Cambridge University Press, 2000)

———, *The Politics*, ed. by Stephen Everson (Cambridge: Cambridge University Press, 1988)

St Augustine, *Concerning the City of God against the Pagans*, trans. by Henry Bettenson (Harmondsworth: Penguin, 1984)

Boccaccio, Giovanni, *Trattatello in laude di Dante*, ed. by Bruno Maier (Milan: Rizzoli, 1965)

Bruni, Leonardo, *Le vite di Dante e del Petrarca*, ed. by Antonio Lanza (Rome: Archivio Guido Izzi, 1987)

Dante Alighieri, *La Commedia secondo l'antica vulgata*, ed. by Giorgio Petrocchi, 2nd edn, 4 vols (Florence: Le Lettere, 1994)

———, *Convivio*, ed. by Cesare Vasoli and Domenico De Robertis, in *Opere minori*, I. ii

———, *Dantis Alagherii Epistolae: The Letters of Dante*, ed. by Paget Toynbee, 2nd edn (Oxford: Clarendon Press, 1966)

———, *De vulgari eloquentia*, ed. and trans. by Steven Botterill (Cambridge: Cambridge University Press 1996)

———, *De vulgari eloquentia*, ed. by Pier Vincenzo Mengaldo, in *Opere minori*, II, 1-237

———, *Epistole*, ed. by Arsenio Frugoni and Giorgio Brugnoli, in *Opere minori*, II, 505-643

———, *Monarchia*, ed. and trans. by Prue Shaw (Cambridge: Cambridge University Press, 1996)

———, *Monarchia*, ed. by Bruno Nardi, in *Opere minori*, II, 239-503

———, *Monarchy and Three Political Letters*, trans. by Donald Nicholl and Colin Hardie (London: Weidenfeld and Nicolson, 1954)

———, *Opere minori*, 2 vols (Milan and Naples: Ricciardi, 1979-88)

———, *Quaestio de acqua et terra*, ed. by Francesco Mazzoni, in *Opere minori*, II, 691-880

———, *Vita nuova*, ed. by Domenico De Robertis, in *Opere minori*, I. i, 1-247

Jerusalem Bible (London: Darton, Longman and Todd, 1974)

Latini, Brunetto, *Li livres dou Tresor*, ed. by Francis J. Carmody (Berkeley: University of California Press, 1948)

Lucan, *The Civil War (Pharsalia)*, trans. by J. D. Duff (Cambridge, MA: Harvard University Press; London: Heinemann, 1928)

Ovid, *Metamorphoses*, trans. by Mary M. Innes (Harmondsworth: Penguin, 1955)

Paul the Deacon, *History of the Lombards*, trans. by William Dudley Foulke, ed. by Edward Peters (Philadelphia: University of Pennsylvania Press, 1974)

Paulus Orosius, *The Seven Books of History Against the Pagans*, trans. by Roy J. Deferrari (Washington, DC: Catholic University of America Press, 1964)

Petrarca, Francesco, *Canzoniere*, ed. by Gianfranco Contini (Turin: Einaudi, 1964)

Uguccione da Pisa, *Derivationes*, ed. by Enzo Cecchini and others, 2 vols (Florence: SISMEL/Edizioni del Galluzzo, 2004)

Villani, Giovanni, *Nuova cronica*, ed. by Giuseppe Porta, 3 vols (Parma: Guanda, 1990-91)

Virgil, trans. by H. Rushton Fairclough, 2 vols (Cambridge, MA: Harvard University Press; London: Heinemann, 1916)

Virgil, *Eclogues*, in *Virgil*, I, 2-77

Virgil, *Georgics*, in *Virgil*, I, 80-237

Virgil, *The Aeneid*, trans. by W. F. Jackson Knight (Harmondsworth: Penguin, 1956)

Secondary Sources

Ahern, John, 'Epistles', in Lansing, ed., *The Dante Encyclopedia*, pp. 352-55

Barański, Zygmunt G., '*Comedìa*: Notes on Dante, the Epistle to Cangrande and Medieval Comedy', *Lectura Dantis*, 8 (Spring 1991), 26-55

Barnes, John C., 'Vestiges of the Liturgy in Dante's Verse', in *Dante and the Middle Ages*, ed. by John C. Barnes and Cormac Ó Cuilleanáin (Dublin: Irish Academic Press, 1995), pp. 231-69

Barolini, Teodolinda, *Dante's Poets: Textuality and Truth in the 'Comedy'* (Princeton: Princeton University Press, 1984)

———, 'For the Record: The Epistle to Cangrande and Various "American Dantisti" ', *Lectura Dantis*, 6 (Spring 1990), 140-43

Bemrose, Stephen, *A New Life of Dante* (Exeter: Exeter University Press, 2000)

Bowsky, William M., *Henry VII in Italy: The Conflict of Empire and City-State, 1310-1313* (Lincoln: University of Nebraska Press, 1960)

Brugnoli, Giorgio, 'Introduzione alle *Epistole*', in Dante Alighieri, *Opere minori*, II, 512-21

Cassell, Anthony K., 'Monarchia', in Lansing, ed., *The Dante Encyclopedia*, pp. 616-23

Cosmo, Umberto, *Vita di Dante*, 3rd edn, ed. by Bruno Maier (Florence: La Nuova Italia, 1965)

Deane, Herbert A., *The Political Ideas of St Augustine* (New York and London: Columbia University Press, 1963)

D'Entrèves, A. P., *Dante as a Political Thinker* (Oxford: Clarendon Press, 1952)

Di Scipio, Giuseppe, *The Presence of Pauline Thought in the Works of Dante* (Lewiston, Queenston, and Lampeter: Edwin Mellen Press, 1995)

Dougherty, James, *The Fivesquare City: the City in the Religious Imagination* (Notre Dame and London: Notre Dame University Press, 1980)

Ferrante, Joan, *The Political Vision of the 'Divine Comedy'* (Princeton: Princeton University Press, 1984)

Hall, Ralph G. and Madison U. Sowell, '*Cursus* in the Can Grande Epistle: A Forger Shows His Hand', *Lectura Dantis*, 5 (Fall 1989), 89-104

Hollander, Robert, *Dante: A Life in Works* (New Haven and London: Yale University Press, 2001)

——, *Dante's Epistle to Cangrande* (Ann Arbor: University of Michigan Press, 1993)

Honess, Claire E., 'Dante and Political Poetry in the Vernacular', in *Dante and his Literary Precursors: Twelve Essays*, ed. by John C. Barnes and Jennifer Petrie (Dublin: Four Courts Press, 2007), pp. 117-51

———, *From Florence to the Heavenly City: The Poetry of Citizenship in Dante* (London: Legenda, 2006)

Keen, Catherine, 'Addressing the City: Urban Inclusion/Exclusion in Medieval Italian Exile Lyrics', in *Urban Witness: The Languages of the Medieval Italian Commune*, ed. by Stephen Milner and Nigel Vincent (Leiden: Brill, forthcoming)

———, *Dante and the City* (Stroud: Tempus, 2003)

Kelly, Henry A., *Tragedy and Comedy from Dante to Pseudo-Dante* (Berkeley, Los Angeles, and London: University of California Press, 1989)

Lansing, Richard, ed., *The Dante Encyclopedia* (New York and London: Garland, 2000)

Larner, John, *Italy in the Age of Dante and Petrarch, 1216-1380* (London and New York: Longman, 1980)

Martines, Lauro, 'Political Violence in the Thirteenth Century', in *Violence and Civil Disorder in Italian Cities,* ed. by Lauro Martines (Berkeley, Los Angeles, and London: University of California Press, 1972), pp. 331-53

Martinez, Ronald, 'Dante's Jeremiads: The Fall of Jerusalem and the Burden of the New Pharisees, the Capetians and Florence', in *Dante for the New Millennium,* ed. by Teodolinda Barolini and H. Wayne Storey (New York: Fordham University Press, 2003), pp. 301-19

Matter, E. Ann, *'The Voice of My Beloved': The Song of Songs in Medieval Christianity* (Philadelphia: University of Pennsylvania Press, 1990);

Mazzoni, Francesco, 'Le epistole di Dante', in *Conferenze aretine, 1965* (Arezzo: Zelli, 1966), pp. 47-100

Mazzotta, Giuseppe, *Dante, Poet of the Desert: History and Allegory in the 'Divine Comedy'* (Princeton: Princeton University Press, 1979)

———, *Dante's Vision and the Circle of Knowledge* (Princeton: Princeton University Press, 1993)

———, 'Life of Dante', in *The Cambridge Companion to Dante*, ed. by Rachel Jacoff, 2nd edn (Cambridge: Cambridge University Press, 2007), pp. 1-13

Mineo, Nicolò, 'Mondo classico e città terrena in Dante', in *Dante: un sogno di armonia terrena*, 2 vols (Turin: Tirrenia, 2005), I, 53-85

———, 'Profetismo e apocalittica in Dante: Strutture e temi profetico-apocalittici' in *Dante dalla 'Vita Nuova' alla 'Divina Commedia'* (Catania: Università di Catania, Facoltà di Lettere e Filosofia, 1968)

Moore, Edward, *Studies in Dante*, IV (Oxford: Clarendon Press, 1917)

Morghen, Raffaello, 'Dante profeta', in *Dante profeta*, pp. 139-57

———, *Dante profeta: tra la storia e l'eterno* (Milan: Jaca Book, 1983)

———, 'La lettera di Dante ai Cardinali italiani', in *Dante profeta*, pp. 109-38

——— 'Le lettere politiche di Dante: Testimonianza della sua vita in esilio', in *Dante profeta*, pp. 89-107

Nardi, Bruno, 'Dante profeta', in *Dante e la cultura medievale*, 2nd edn (Bari: Laterza, 1949), pp. 336-416

Nasti, Paola, *Favole d'amore e 'saver profondo': La tradizione salomonica in Dante* (Ravenna: Longo, 2007)

Paolucci, Henry, ed., *The Political Writings of St Augustine* (Chicago: Henry Regnery, 1962)

Pastore Stocchi, Manlio, 'Epistole', in *Enciclopedia dantesca*, ed. by Umberto Bosco and others, 5 vols and Appendix (Rome: Istituto della Enciclopedia Italiana, 1970-78), II, 703-10

Pertile, Lino, '*Canto-cantica-Comedìa* e l'Epistola a Cangrande', *Lectura Dantis*, 9 (Fall 1991), 105-23

——, 'Dante Looks Forward and Back: Political Allegory in the Epistles', *Dante Studies*, 115 (1997), 1-17

——, *La puttana e il gigante: Dal Cantico dei cantici al Paradiso Terrestre di Dante* (Ravenna: Longo, 1998)

Petrocchi, Giorgio, *Vita di Dante* (Bari: Laterza, 1983)

Salvemini, Gaetano, *Magnati e popolani in Firenze dal 1280 al 1295* (Turin: Einaudi, 1960)

Schnapp, Jeffrey T., *The Transfiguration of History at the Center of Dante's 'Paradise'* (Princeton: Princeton University Press, 1986)

Scott, John A., *Dante's Political Purgatory* (Philadelphia: University of Pennsylvania Press, 1996)

——, *Understanding Dante* (Notre Dame: University of Notre Dame Press, 2004)

Waley, Daniel, *The Italian City Republics*, 3rd edn (London and New York: Longman, 1988)

MHRA Critical Texts

This series aims to provide affordable critical editions of lesser-known literary texts that are not in print or are difficult to obtain. The texts will be taken from the following languages: English, French, German, Italian, Portuguese, Russian, and Spanish. Titles will be selected by members of the distinguished Editorial Board and edited by leading academics. The aim is to produce scholarly editions rather than teaching texts, but the potential for crossover to undergraduate reading lists is recognized. The books will appeal both to academic libraries and individual scholars.

Malcolm Cook
Chairman, Editorial Board

Editorial Board

Professor John Batchelor (English)
Professor Malcolm Cook (French) (*Chairman*)
Professor Ritchie Robertson (Germanic)
Professor Derek Flitter (Spanish)
Professor Brian Richardson (Italian)
Dr Stephen Parkinson (Portuguese)
Professor David Gillespie (Slavonic)

Published titles

1. *Odilon Redon, 'Écrits'* (edited by Claire Moran, 2005)

2. *Les Paraboles Maistre Alain en Françoys* (edited by Tony Hunt, 2005)

3. *Letzte Chancen: Vier Einakter von Marie von Ebner-Eschenbach* (edited by Susanne Kord, 2005)

4. *Macht des Weibes: Zwei historische Tragödien von Marie von Ebner-Eschenbach* (edited by Susanne Kord, 2005)

5. *A Critical Edition of 'La tribu indienne; ou, Édouard et Stellina' by Lucien Bonaparte* (edited by Cecilia Feilla, 2006)

6. *Dante Alighieri, 'Four Political Letters'* (translated and with a commentary by Claire E. Honess, 2007)

(continues overleaf)

7. *'La Disme de Penitanche'* by Jehan de Journi (edited by Glynn Hesketh, 2006)

8. *'François II, roi de France'* by Charles-Jean-François Hénault (edited by Thomas Wynn, 2006)

10. *La Peyrouse dans l'Isle de Tahiti, ou le Danger des Présomptions: drame politique* (edited by John Dunmore, 2006)

Forthcoming titles

9. *Istoire de la Chastelaine du Vergier et de Tristan le Chevalier* (edited by Jean-François Kosta-Théfaine)

11. *Casimir Britannicus. English Paraphrases and Emulations of the Poetry of Maciej Kazimierz Sarbiewski* (edited by Piotr Urbański and Krzysztof Fordoński)

12. *'La Devineresse ou les faux enchantements'* by Jean Donneau de Visé and Thomas Corneille (edited by Julia Prest)

13. *'Phosphorus Hollunder' und 'Der Posten der Frau' von Louise von François* (edited by Barbara Burns)

14. *Le Gouvernement present, ou éloge de son Eminence, satyre ou la Miliade* (edited by Paul Scott)

15. *Ovide du remede d'amours* (edited by Tony Hunt)

For details of how to order please visit our website at www.criticaltexts.mhra.org.uk